A MANUAL ON ETCHING AND ENGRAVING GLASS

A MANUAL ON ETCHING AND ENGRAVING GLASS

G. M. HEDDLE

M. COLL. H. (HONS.)

LONDON / ALEC TIRANTI / 1971

1st edition 1961
Reprinted 1971

PRINTED BY SUTTONS (PAIGNTON) LTD.
BOUND BY C. & H. T. EVANS OF CROYDON

© *Copyright 1971 Alec Tiranti Ltd., 72 Charlotte Street, London W.1*

Made and printed in the United Kingdom

CLOTH: ISBN 0 85458—978/3   PAPER: ISBN 0 85458—986/4

CONTENTS

page

Foreword - - - - - - - - 1

Permissions and photographs - - - - - 4

Introduction and acknowledgements - - - - 5

I. HISTORICAL BACKGROUND - - - - 7

II. DESIGNING A PIECE OF GLASS
   AND ITS DECORATION - - - - - 22

   Decorative processes p.23
   The qualities of glass p.24

III. MAKING A HANDMADE BLOWN GLASS VESSEL 28

   The making of the metal p.28
   The making of the blown vessel p.30

IV. ETCHING GLASS - - - - - - - 33

   Acid finishes for glassware p.33
   Preparing the blank for single-tone etching p.34
   Etching the blank p.35
   French embossing or multi-tone etching p.37
   Post etching processes p.37
   Mass production of designs by acid etching p.38
   The acid treatment of flashed glasses p.39

V. ENGRAVING GLASS BY DIAMOND POINT - 40

VI. ENGRAVING GLASS BY COPPER WHEEL - - 42

   Surface wheel engraving; carving in low relief p.43
   Carving in high relief p.46

VII. OTHER FORMS OF DECORATION -   -   -   49

         Sandblasting p.49
         Enamelling p.51
         Painting p.51
         Staining p.52
         Cutting p.52
         Intaglio p.54
         Cameo cutting p.54
         Pressing p.55

Glossary of terms used in the glass industry -   -   -   56

Notes to illustrations -   -   -   -   -   -   -   61

FOREWORD

by

W. J. Wilson

F.S.I.A.

Managing Director and Chief Designer of
JAMES POWELL & SONS (WHITEFRIARS) LTD.

A CYNIC ONCE REMARKED that 'history is one damned thing after another.' This prompts me to the happier reflection that the history of glass has been one beautiful thing after another : a crescendo of loveliness through the ages, a symphony of glory that has almost certainly not yet reached its highest note. Craftsmanship in glass is still vibrant today as, sadly, in too few industries. Moreover, new technical skills of the machine age are helping to produce the inimitable handiwork of the craftsman in profitable quantities.

The date of the first appearance of glass, in my opinion the most fascinating material created by man, is not precisely known. Originally glass was fashioned not for its own delightful sake but as a glaze for clay beads and other ornaments of the Egyptians some 5,000 years ago. Much later, glass vessels were fabricated by the laborious sand-core method until, at the beginning of the Christian era, the introduction of the blowing iron brought what was probably the greatest step forward in the story of glassmaking. This advance was as momentous to man the aesthete as the earlier discovery of the wheel had been to practical man, thus emancipated from the cumbersome sledge. The way was now open for craftsmen of Imperial Rome and Syria to express in tangible form mankind's undying worship of beauty— expressions in glass that cannot be equalled for beauty and intricate work today.

I refuse to believe that these craftsmen of the time of Christ, expressing man's fight for loveliness among the tyrannies and bloodshed of their merciless era, were directed by any designer. To be sure they were artists and craftsmen in their own right, expressing mankind's immortal desire for beauty without thought for profit and untroubled by sordid anxieties about the 'rate for the job.' To them, talent was more than talents.

1

Crocodile tears sufficient to fill the most monumental vase are shed nowadays in the Press and in after-dinner speeches mourning dying craftsmanship. Would those who weep at its passing smile at its resurrection, bearing in mind the price that must nowadays be paid for craftsmanship? The craftsman in industry, like the mechanic and the man who sweeps the floor, must earn his costly living. There is only one way to preserve the age-old traditions of craftsmanship in glass in our modern society; and that is by paying the piper—he still pipes a lovely tune, but it comes expensive.

If, as I have surmised, the old masters of Rome and Syria worked without benefit of designer, that functionary is very much in evidence in a modern glassworks. Rightly so, if the happiest results are to be obtained when a large, repetitive production is involved. Few good craftsmen are also good designers. It is nevertheless true that where individual pieces are concerned, works of genius (as with all forms of art) are forthcoming only when artist and craftsman are—as so rarely —dual spirits united in one body. Such is fortunately the case where the decoration of glass, by the methods discussed by Geoffrey Heddle in this book, is concerned.

The student designer, aiming to produce magnificent pieces of table or decorative glassware, is at a disadvantage in his apprentice efforts. Because it is bulky, expensive to melt and needing much ancillary equipment, glass for training purposes is hard to come by. Not so for the engraver. Armed only with a diamond-point pencil, a piece of glass, and a cushion for use as a dark backcloth and resting place, the aspiring tyro can practise to his heart's content in the seclusion of his own home. His fumbling efforts can be destroyed, unseen by sardonic eye, until that ever-glorious day when he first realizes that his hand has found its cunning, his eye its command. This applies also to wheel-engraving—although not so simply. A great deal of training is required to master this technique, which is nevertheless taught with facility in a number of art schools. Many students have set up lathes at home and have, within a comparatively short time, been able to produce beautiful work on a free-lance basis—to their own profit and the enrichment of their patrons. *O! si sic omnia.*

Just as craftsmanship shines out from a vase or a goblet, so from this book's pages it is instantly apparent that Mr. Heddle has been at immense pains to bring together by word and illustration all that is likely to interest those who humbly admire England's rich heritage of etched and engraved glass. Such a survey, to the best of my knowledge, has never before been attempted. That it should at its first attempt have so eminently succeeded is a tribute to its author, a tribute which I am honoured to endorse in this foreword. This book should be of great service to the would-be student glass decorator. It will also benefit and interest others who cannot themselves attempt, much less succeed in, this high form of craftsmanship, but who nevertheless wish to worship at the shrine of English etched and engraved glass. They also serve art who only stand and gaze in awe.

WILLIAM J. WILSON

PERMISSIONS

Dorothy Brown, D.A.(EDIN.)	27.
Central Press Photos Ltd.	35, 36, 37.
Council of Industrial Design	4, 5, 77, 78, 79.
E. M. Dinkel, R.W.S.	82, 83.
J. C. Downing, A.R.C.A., F.R.S.A.	80, 81.
Edinburgh Crystal Glass Co. Ltd.	7.
Hans Erni	66, 67, 68.
Glass Manufacturers' Federation	41, 51, 85.
Rupert Hart-Davis Ltd. (from Laurence Whistler, *Engraved Glass 1952-1958*).	52, 53, 54, 55, 56, 57.
Holmegaards Glasvaerk a/s.	31.
Karhula — Iittala	29, 42.
Keystone Press Agency Ltd.	10.
Manchester City Art Gallery	34.
N. V. Koninklijke Nederlandsche Glasfabriek	23, 40, 69.
Aktiebolaget Orrefors Glasbruk	28, 73, 74, 76.
D. B. Peace, A.R.I.B.A., A.M.T.P.I.	24, 25, 26, 33.
A. L. Pope, A.R.C.A., A.R.E.	60, 61, 62.
Stephen Rickard, A.R.B.S.	71, 72, 84.
S.A.L.I.R. (Studio 'Ars Labor' Industrie Riuniti), Italy	30, 70.
Äse Voss Schrader	32.
Steuben Glass	14, 15, 16, 17, 18, 19, 20, 21, 22, 58, 75, .
Stevens & Williams Ltd.	43, 44, 45, 46, 47, 48, 49, 50.
Stourbridge Glass Co. Ltd.	6.
Stuart & Sons	8, 9.
THE TIMES	63.
Topical Press Agency Ltd.	64, 65.
E. J. Webster, DES.R.C.A.	11, 12, 13.
W. J. Wilson, F.S.I.A.	1, 2, 3.
H. Warren Wilson	59.

PHOTOGRAPHS

W. D. Betts	38, 39, 86.
H. Cartwright	43, 44, 45, 46, 47, 48, 49, 50.
H. Tempest (Commercial) Ltd.	26.

INTRODUCTION AND ACKNOWLEDGMENTS

FOR MANY HUNDREDS of years glass has been known to, and used by, man. In common with numerous other materials, glass has been used for purely utilitarian and for decorative purposes. Often the utilitarian glass articles have been decorated. It is with this last fact that this book deals.

With the development of man's knowledge and technical skills, various methods of decoration have been developed. Decoration may be effected firstly, in the integral colour and shaping during the manufacture of the article. Secondly, decoration may be effected after manufacture, by the use of abrasives, chemicals and adhesives.

As in other crafts, the extent and form of the decoration used in and on glass has been regulated, in the main, by fashion. Cut-glass has been in fashion for countless years, and it is likely to be so for countless years more. Glass decorated in other ways, such as by diamond- or steel-point engraving, or copper-wheel engraving, is, however, enjoying a renaissance; and methods such as etching and sandblasting are becoming increasingly popular.

The object of this book is to describe the methods of acid etching, and diamond-point and copper-wheel engraving, which are used by the artists of today, and about which little has been written. In addition, an outline is given of other decorative treatments, upon which much has been written.

These three methods depend for their effect upon the obscuration of the transparent glass, the surface of which is naturally very shiny, or has been mechanically or chemically polished. The obscuration has a matt white appearance, but has a very different texture for each different technique, which has its own characteristic appearance, as will be seen from the photographs. Obscuration is achieved in etching by permitting the shape of the design to be eaten onto and into the glass by suitable acids. In diamond-point and steel-point engraving, the surface of the glass is scratched or stippled, whereas in copper-wheel engraving the surface of the glass is ground away. In all three methods the depth to which the glass is removed is intimately related to the feeling of form obtained in the design. Hence, one method is achieved chemically, and the other two, respectively, manually and mechanically by abrasion.

5

The material in the chapters of the various decorative techniques has been gathered from many independent, or free-lance artist-craftsmen in this country, who have been generous enough to help me, discuss with me, demonstrate for me, and answer my numerous questions about the different techniques which they employ in their craft. Among those whom I wish to thank specially are David B. Peace, Dorothy Brown, Stephen Rickard and Anthony L. Pope, all of whom are members of the Craft Centre of Great Britain.

I wish also to thank W. J. Wilson, Laurence Whistler and Peter C. Goodall for their greatly valued help to me when writing this book. The material dealing with the production of glass and the making of a glass vessel was obtained during visits to the long-established and famous glassworks of James Powell & Sons (Whitefriars) Ltd.

The information for the chapters dealing with the history of glass-making and its decoration has been obtained by work done in the Victoria and Albert Museum and British Museum. The permanent exhibition of historical and technical aspects of glassmaking and decoration, and the library at the headquarters of the Glass Manufacturers' Federation have been very helpful. In addition I acknowledge permission given by Penguin Books Ltd., to use some material from *Glass through the Ages* by Barrington Haynes.

Included in this book are a few photographs of Scandinavian, European and American work. I hope that they will be of themselves a suitable yardstick with which to measure the quality of English work.

I must emphasise that I have not attempted to write a complete manual for the craftsman. The ability to produce work of the quality illustrated herein, cannot be attained by reading a book, but is, rather, an aptitude developed by years of hard training and much practice to acquire the practical craft skills and artistic ability. These must be combined with a training in the appreciation and understanding of the many natures of the material which control the decoration of it. This book is written as an introductory explanation and statement of the modern movement to produce decorated glass, and also to give the general reader a background story of these forms of decorated glass which are becoming increasingly popular.

CHAPTER ONE

HISTORICAL BACKGROUND

THIS CHAPTER is not intended to be a comprehensive account of a product known to man, and made by him for nearly 5,000 years. I propose to put forward very briefly a simple account of the generally accepted history of glass-making and its decoration in the Western Hemisphere, that is, West of its birthplace—Egypt.

The earliest glass was made by Nature. Nature's greyish natural glass, as found in the Glass Mountain of Yellowstone National Park, U.S.A., is called Obsidian.

Pliny, writing in the first century A.D. describes how merchants, encamped on the sands of the river Belus,* placed their cooking pots on some of the cakes of natron they were transporting. In the morning they found that the sand and soda (natron) had fused together forming glass. This story is most probably a myth because the temperature at which sand and soda fuses is about 1,500 degrees centigrade. It is certain that the product looked nothing like the modern conception of glass.

The earliest man-made glass was produced by Egyptians at some date prior to 3,000 B.C. The natural resources of the country then proffered abundant sand, natron lakes (for the soda) and acacia groves (wood for the fuel). The glass at that time was what we would call a glaze, and was used to coat articles, or to be cast. With the passing of time man discovered that the glaze could be made thick enough to support itself, and he used it for making trinkets and inlay work, including mosaics. Around 1300 B.C. the Egyptians evolved a process in which a moulded sand core was repeatedly dipped into molten glaze, and withdrawn in order to allow the glaze to harden, and then when a sufficiently thick coat had been obtained, the sand core was removed to leave a glass pot or jar. Between 1300 B.C. and 50 B.C. press moulding was developed.

The most outstanding advance in glassmaking was the discovery

*The River Belus flows into the Mediterranean not far from Acre in Israel.

about 50 B.C. of the technique of blowing glass. Some unusually enterprising Egyptian must have substituted a hollow iron rod for the solid one which was used to hold the sand core, and found that if after gathering a blob of glass at one end, he blew down from the other, the blob would become a bubble. The tools he used to fashion this bubble have changed very little in character since then. The Alexandrians introduced the art of drawing on glass with a graving tool, which was in effect line engraving, and also cutting and carving glass, which left designs in line and relief. Cameo carving or engraving is carried out on material which is either natural—such as stone, or artificial—such as glass, having two layers of different colours. The uppermost layer is partially removed, so utilising the second layer as a background. The Portland Vase is the most outstanding example still in existence of cameo work, and was carried out by Roman craftsmen in a later period. The Alexandrians must have had a thorough knowledge of their metals (the glassmaker's name for glass) as they had to ensure that the metals for their cameos had the same coefficient of expansion. The white was partially cut away leaving a white design in relief on a blue base metal. Rome, Palestine, Cyprus and Crete had, by this time, well established glasshouses of their own. Craftsmen obviously travelled along the trade routes, and the spread of the Roman Empire allowed them to do so freely. The glassmakers moved to fresh markets when previous ones were satisfied. The spread of knowledge was also accentuated by the fact that the timber used for fuel was periodically worked out at the established area of manufacture and the glassmakers had to move to a new site for fresh supplies of fuel. The glassmaking industry was therefore nomadic, and remained so until the fifteenth century. Glasshouses were set up in the Rhône valley, Spain, North Africa, and the Seine and Rhine valleys, and with the arrival of the Romans in England, glassmaking was carried out at Colchester and Faversham.

All of the glass of the first four centuries is termed Roman, not because it was made by Romans but because it was made in the era of Roman domination. The glass was usually of the simplest style and consisted chiefly of plates, dishes, bowls, beakers and bottles. Stemmed vessels were introduced and because of their delicacy and scarcity became fashionable toward the end of this period. The Romans introduced gold-leaf decoration both applied to the surface of the vessel and also sandwiched between two layers of clear metal.

Following the decline in power of the Roman Empire, the countries of Europe and North Africa were beset with invaders and civil strife for four hundred years or more and learning suffered considerably, no less than did the art, knowledge and craftsmanship of glassmaking and decoration. However, those already well established glassmaking and decorating centres, such as Rome, Ravenna, Pisa and Aquila persisted to produce fine ware as and when possible under changing circumstances, but they eventually succumbed to the apathetic attitude of the times. The official adoption of Christianity by Rome in A.D. 342 had started a steady decline in trade for those craftsmen who made glass vases in which the pagans buried the ashes of their dead. This practice ceased with the spread of Christianity throughout Italy. Paganism still lingered in the northern countries and its market for glassware lingered with it until the eighth century, when it too disappeared. Tableglass for the poor and rich alike was still being produced in quantity in the central and northern European countries. The style and decoration depended upon the price which could be fetched. Fine glass was produced in Syria and, with Egyptian glass, was marketed in Constantinople, where ornate articles always found a ready buyer. The colouring of the metal, the trailing and prunting of the ware for decoration and also the cutting of the ware, was carried out to a large extent in the Islamic style, rather than styles influenced by Rome.

From 800 to 1400 is generally known as the Empty Age in the History of Glass. It is so called because there is a dearth of specimens remaining to us, because fragile glass articles were very prone to destruction during the invasions and wars which occurred in northern Europe. Semitic glassmakers migrated to Altare in Montferrat, not for from Genoa, because of the break-up of Charlemagne's empire. The migration there of the Normandy-Picardy craftsmen coincides with the establishment, after years of war, of the Duchy of Normandy (911-1204). The people who remained in the old centres of glassmaking tried to continue the manufacture of glass but found it impossible, for the knowledge and skill to do so had gone with the craftsmen. Only *verre de fougère*, a potash glass made with bracken ash as an alkali, was produced in small quantities for a very poor local market. *Waldglas* a *verre de fougère*, made in the southern Germanic countries, was made with beech wood ash instead of bracken ash. The fine glass used by royalty in northern Europe was probably brought from the East, or after 1300 was made by straggling glassmakers migrating back from Altare.

Laurence Vitrearius, probably an Altarist, settled and made bracken glass vessels and window-glass, near Chiddingfold, in the Surrey-Sussex Weald in 1226. Vitrearius was the first glassmaker known by name in England.

The Schurterre family came to England in 1343 and specialised in stained glass for windows. The specialised industry of window-glass making somewhat restricted the manufacture of vessel-glass both in this country and in Europe. Comfort came before convenience, which is a reason for the dearth of glassware in this period.

In Syria mould-blown patterned glass was made and the decoration of glass included cutting and wheel engraving : the latter was of very simple patterns or naturalistic designs. The Crusades, which took place at this time, did much to hinder the development of Syrian glass; and in fact the craftsmen were driven into the interior of the country, especially to Damascus, where they again produced fine glass, enamelling being a speciality. Techniques were improved and very fine glassware was made up to the end of the fourteenth century, when Tamerlane invaded the country and carried off her craftsmen. The Venetians seized this opportunity to increase their trade and also develop their own techniques.

In the thirteenth century, Venice, Altare, Padua and Bologna were producing fine glass. The craftsmen of Murano, the suburb of Venice where the glasshouses were situated, went to Altare in the fourteenth century because of warring in their State. This provided exchange of ideas, as happened between trading ports of different countries, and the individual styles were also often copied.

In 1224 Venice boasted a Glassblowers' Guild, which in a short time monopolised the European industry because it enforced severe penalties on any craftsman who left the area or even gave away trade secrets. The quality of the products gradually rose, and by the end of the fourteenth century the craftsmen exported vessels to the Low Countries and England. In the absence of Syrian competition the Venetians took quite a long time to develop their techniques in enamelling and fashioning, but this led to a distinctive style of their own and the products lost their *façon de Syrie*. Purely Venetian glass was made from about 1450, by which time the craftsmen had mastered the colouring of the metal, the making of clear metal and also enamelling and gilding. In the fifteenth, sixteenth and seventeenth centuries the techniques of blowing and fashioning glass vessels, such as plates, bowls, jugs, bottles and wineglasses were developed to, perhaps, their highest level. The walls of the bowls of the glasses were blown very delicately thin and the stems were drawn to extremely fragile dimensions. These techniques they began later to flaunt as the blowers displayed their superb and unsurpassed skill in their craft. Decoration was in the form of coloured cords inside the glass, coloured trails, enamelling, gilding, cutting and both forms of engraving. The diamond-point engraving was perhaps the most prominent due to the fact that the walls of the 'ware were so very thin. Diamond-point engraving in its true, glorious form originated in Venice in the first half of the sixteenth century. The chief characteristic, until the seventeenth century was well advanced, was that the lines did not cross. Cross hatching, produced later, aimed at giving greater intensity of light and shade, in competition with the appearance of wheel-engraving, introduced in Prague a few years before the end of the sixteenth century. Due to territorial losses there was a decline in trade in the latter part of the seventeenth century. Exports dwindled and the industry began to deal more extensively with mirror, plate and chandelier glass. A short-lived revival in the early eighteenth century concluded at the end of the century with the fall of the Republic, and the present revival began at the beginning of the second half of the nineteenth century.

The revival of glassmaking in western Europe began between the beginning and the middle of the thirteenth century. The actual institutors of the revival were perhaps some Altarists who returned to their ancestral home in Normandy. However, a general spread northward of craftsmen from Altare brought back the industry to now more settled and prosperous countries.

Very little is known of the thirteenth, fourteenth and fifteenth century western European glass. The glass made was better than the *verre de fougère* and *waldglas*, but it is not likely that it was any better than the Venetian glass of the same period. Window glass was the main product at the beginning of the revival and utility vessels became a side line. These utility vessels also had an order of importance, namely, lamp oil containers, phials, bottles and lastly drinking glasses. The style was mediaeval until after 1450, when it tended to become *à la façon de Venise*.

The revival of German glass began with the setting up of small glasshouses along the trade routes of the south in the late fifteenth and sixteenth centuries, and it reached the north in the late seventeenth century. The style was naturally Venetian but there was a definite attempt to be original, which unhappily usually spoilt the design of the 'ware. The metal was usually tinted and enamel was applied in harmony with the tint of the base metal. This enamelling was robustly executed and of high quality. The German enamelled commemorative glassware was probably, and perhaps still remains, the best in the world. When the tinted ware died out in favour of colourless metal, the enamelling of glass did not stay long. Diamond-point work captured the fancy of the precise Germans. The Rhinelanders produced quantities of diamond-point work, the designs of which suited the shapes of the blanks and were executed in very free lines. Painting and enamelling were the most popular forms of decoration, with large quantities of wheel-engraving produced as well. Acid work was started in Germany at the end of the seventeenth century.

Spain, however, did not develop her glassmaking, and most of her glassware was imported from the eagerly competing suppliers of England, Holland and Germany. Spanish glassmaking, which at one time had suffered at the hands of and later had been encouraged by the Moors, was nevertheless very good, and Barcelona, famous for its rich green enamelling, might have equalled Venice. France failed to continue her traditional glass industry and instead went over to the industries of agriculture and war. Only a relatively localised industry was carried out in Burgundy and Normandy.

In Belgium the chief glassmaking centres were Antwerp and Liège. Although the glassmakers followed the *façon de Venise,* each had his own individuality. The trade of Antwerp fell to British competition at the end of the seventeenth century, and Liège continued alone.

In Holland the industry was localised. In quality and style it followed closely the pattern of the other countries. The most popular and traditional product was the *roemer,* the improvement in design of which was great. The improvement in metal used was also extensive. The Dutch, however, were glass lovers more than glassmakers, which was perhaps due to the lack of fuel which, as will have been noted, was still wood. Their love of beautiful glass led the Dutch to make an industry of the decoration of other countries' glass, often English because of its quality. Hence from the last quarter of the seventeenth century the Dutch applied themselves to engraving first with the diamond, using lines only, and then with the wheel. This decoration added greatly to the beauty of what was, before, probably a glass of no great account. The designs were executed with the utmost skill and artistic ability; the form the designs usually took was that of a commemorative motif of some type. These pieces were therefore usually commissioned by a rich patron. To the Dutch it was a matter of tradition that on special occasions such as weddings, anniversaries, etc., they offered one another crystal glass bearing an inscription or appropriate motto. A coat of arms, a portrait, or a scene usually accompanied the inscription.

Although in 1646 Anna Roemers Visscher line-engraved a glass with a decoration of a cherry, leaves and an inscription, and stipple engraved the shading on the cherry, it is to Frans Greenwood (1680-1761) to whom the honour is given of being the first to use the stipple form of diamond-point engraving. Frans Greenwood certainly placed stipple engraving in an extremely high position as a style of engraving, and his work is distinct from all others who used the diamond point. Greenwood's first piece of work, in 1720, was, in fact, entirely in line, but the rest of his work is carried out totally in stipple, except for a few details such as inscriptions. On some pieces Greenwood made a heavy stipple as a background, and on other pieces he used the stipple for the lighter parts, and left the glass untouched to represent the shadow and darker places. Greenwood engraved decorations of floral, pictorial, caricature, inscription and mainly portrait motifs, of perhaps a more delicate nature than the work of those who followed him. Much of the work was copied from paintings executed by himself and other artists.

Aert Schouman (1710-1792) was the second of the three pre-eminent Dutch diamond-point glass engravers of the eighteenth century. He was probably a friend of Greenwood. His work is of a similar nature to Greenwood's.

David Wolff (1732?-1798?) was the third great Dutch engraver of the time. His work was mainly pictorial. Buckley in his book on Wolff states that it has been suggested on very strong grounds that Wolff used a hammer to tap the sharp, distinct, accurately placed dots in his stippling. The dots of the stipple are distributed more evenly than in the work of any other artist.

These three artists produced work of an exceptionally high pictorial quality.

Hydrofluoric acid was discovered in 1771 by C. Sheile, a Swedish chemist, when he decomposed fluorspar with concentrated sulphuric acid. It is known that acid etching was carried out in The Hague in the 1780's.

The fact that Britain was becoming a Protestant country in the sixteenth century brought religious refugees and, of course, amongst them glassmakers, who gladly made use of both the religious asylum and the developing trade of the Trade Routes. From 1550 onward well equipped glassmakers came to England, of whom Carré, a Lorrainer, and Giacomo Verzelini, a Venetian, were the greatest. Carré obtained a licence in 1567 and set up furnaces in the traditional area, Surrey, at Alford; but broke tradition and established a glasshouse in London, where he intended to make *cristallo*. Pieces of his work, however, show that it was free from bubbles, the workmanship, texture and finish were very good, and the style Altarist. Carré has the honour of having established modern glassmaking in England.

Because of the enlarged Wealden industry, Carré met with considerable opposition both from older established glasshouses, and from the ironworkers of the area. Disputes arose over the amount of wood fuel which was used, and the available resources left. Carré's craftsmen left for the woods of Hampshire, then of Gloucestershire, and on to Eccleshall and Stourbridge in Worcestershire, to Cheswardine in Shropshire and eventually to Newcastle-on-Tyne. This movement to areas where coal is found did not happen entirely by chance, but the glass and iron furnaces of the time used only 'lop and top' wood, suitable only for burning; and the selection of sites cannot be put down to the availability of coal alone. However, in 1611, new furnaces were designed and the glassmakers, unlike the ironmakers, were using coal fuel before the Edict of 1615 which forbade the use of wood as fuel. The Edict eventually exterminated the Wealden industries.

In 1572 Carré died, and Verzelini took over the 'house, but he did not receive a welcome from the English merchants who suspected him. His 'house was burnt down in 1575, whether by accident or design is not known. To protect himself Verzelini secured a royal licence giving him sole right to make Venice glass in England; and it further prohibited the importation of foreign 'ware. This licence was for twenty-one years, and in this time the country assimilated a knowledge of fine glassmaking. Verzelini's style was naturally that of a high-class Venetian but his metal was not up to the standard of Carré's. The five specimens of his work which remain are all diamond-point engraving and the dates on these pieces range between 1580 and 1590. Verzelini's glasses are all characteristically the same in style, type of design, and the manner in which the decoration is executed with the diamond-point. The decoration is of foliage of an eastern, arabesque form, and carried out in line, and line shading only. The form of the decoration is continuous, encircling the bowls of the glasses, and appears similar to German and Venetian decorations of the same period.

The apparent dearth of specimens becomes understandable when it is realised that drinking glasses, likely to be dated, decorated and recognisable, were only a very small part of the output which included the more important kitchen and table 'ware of bottles, bowls, dishes and plates made in foreign *façons*.

Verzelini retired with the expiration of his licence and Sir Jerome Bowes took over from him. Bowes was a soldier-financier with little knowledge of glass, and during the time of his licence, until 1606, little development was made.

Bowes was succeeded by Mansell, who was, in the modern conception of the word, a financier, and like Bowes knew little of the glassmaking at the time he gained control of it. Unlike Bowes, Mansell, during the forty years of his office, developed glassmaking from an unstable, scattered art into a genuine industry. New licences were obtained which prohibited the importation of foreign glass, although some came into the country by devious means. As Mansell was a financier and industrialist, he made glass for the consumer; utility was of prime importance, and aesthetic appeal was generally a secondary consideration. However, Mansell had the skilled craftsmen, the high quality metal and a ready market, so it may safely be assumed that some high quality drinking vessels were produced. During the Civil War and Commonwealth regime Mansell lost control of his monopoly, and glassmaking and blowing were done when and where possible. Sir Robert Mansell died in 1656. The then very popular and now famous enamelling was carried out by the Beilby family in the Newcastle area.

In 1638 Charles I granted a charter to the Glass Sellers' Company, which was formed the year before as a protest against the 'badness of Mansell's glass.' With the return of a monarch as head of the country a new enthusiasm spread throughout the land, and infected the craftsmen and market alike. The G.S.C. controlled the industry by directing what it should make. The second Duke of Buckingham took a prominent part in the glassmaking industry between 1660 and 1674 by financing many craftsmen who cared to work for him, and he gradually gained a hold of practically every glasshouse in the country. Obviously, as the Duke could not keep a personal eye on each 'house, he had to have managers, and it was these managers whom the G.S.C. influenced. The glass made at this time was of high quality in a slight Netherlandish style, and commemorative work was decorated with diamond-point engraving.

Demand for good quality glass was high, and in fact exceeded production. Because of this, John Green, a member of the G.S.C., designed glassware which he contracted to craftsmen at Murano in Italy. Some dissatisfaction arose when the glasses were made to variations of, and not solely according to, the specified designs. The G.S.C. therefore embarked upon a new policy, and selected George Ravenscroft to make a scientific investigation into the possible production of a very high quality metal. Ravenscroft introduced an oxide of lead into the batch and after experiments with the proportions he believed that he had achieved success. The G.S.C. announced that earlier faults were remedied, and in 1677 introduced the 'raven's head' seal as a distinguishing mark. Ravenscroft renewed his agreement with the G.S.C. but soon after gave notice. The seal was quietly dropped when it was found that this new glass began to crizzle (decay). Hawly Bishopp took over the Savoy glasshouse in 1682 and succeeded Ravenscroft as chief scientist.

Bishopp experimented with the proportions of constituents of the batch and finally achieved success. Up to this date Venetian flint pebbles were crushed and used for the silica of crystal metal; English flints were used later, and then it was realised that sand was as useful and flints ceased to be used, although the term 'flint glass' still lingered on. The metal was much clearer than that produced by Ravenscroft. Continental craftsmen thought the glass was good enough to engrave, and did so with both diamond-point and copper-wheel. In 1685 the new lead metal was being made throughout the country and English glass reigned supreme over Europe for a century to follow. Soda glass continued to be made, and the quality of the metal and craftsmanship was up to that of the lead glass.

During the last few years of the seventeenth century foreign cut-glass was being sold in small quantities on the English market. In 1709 the G.S.C. officially disapproved of this and tried to stop the imports. However, in 1713 the Treaty of Utrecht opened the way for trade with Europe, and Bohemian 'ware was imported again. In 1714 George of Hanover came to the English throne and there was an infiltration of German craftsmen into England. By 1719 cut-glass was widely advertised.

There are still in existence many examples of both plain and decorated Jacobite glass. The decoration is carried out by diamond-point and wheel-engraving, the latter form becoming a separate craft in this country for the first time. The designs are in the forms of partially opened and closed rose buds, thistles, portraits, stars and oak-leaves, all of which are said to have definite political meanings. A large number of these, and other decorative designs recording social, political and historical happenings, are accompanied with memorial and commemorative inscriptions and mottoes. Cutting was incorporated on some of the glasses, usually on their stems, made in the second half of the Jacobean period.

In 1745 the Glass Excise Act was introduced, and resulted in the reduction of the weight of glass which was used to make articles, causing them to be made much thinner. Cutting was obviously affected, and it is because of this that much shallower cutting was a necessity. Engraving, naturally, was not affected.

The Excise Act stifled exports and hindered research. The only means of producing and selling glass cheaply was to cut it in order to lessen the weight, and this the craftsmen did in excess compared with modern standards. This was the inception of the English tradition of cut-glass as a form of decoration. By the time the Excise Act was repealed in 1845, Stourbridge craftsmen had set up, and manned, glasshouses in Ireland, where they were exempt from the Excise. Nevertheless, at first they were able to satisfy only the local market, as until 1782 glassware was not allowed to be exported from that country.

In 1825 pressed glass was introduced to the British industry and at first was produced to imitate cut-glass designs. Cut, pressed, engraved and enamelled glass was shown in great quantity at the Great Exhibition of 1851.

In 1862 William Morris founded Morris, Marshall & Faulkner Co., and undertook church decoration, carving, stained-glass, metalwork, paperhangings, chintzes and carpets. Morris did much to bring back good taste in all forms of art. His stained glass was made by James Powell of Whitefriars, London, and undoubtedly he also designed and had made for him table glass as well.

The second half of the nineteenth century saw a grand era of diamond-point, and especially of wheel-engraving, in the Stourbridge area, where, as in Scotland, the use of the engraving wheel was greatly developed. Gradually handblown glass has been ousted by the machine, but each glasshouse of longstanding is still producing quantities of very high quality handmade glass.

In 1935 diamond-point engraving was revived in England, through the work of W. J. Wilson and Laurence Whistler. This delicate craft was brought from Venice in the reign of Queen Elizabeth I, but virtually disappeared after the eighteenth century, having been surpassed by the cruder Dutch and German methods of wheel engraving. Today, most of W. J. Wilson's work is commemorative and he has evolved a style of lettering that is clear and easily read, and combines elegance with virility. His work shows skill and taste in combining the lettering of the inscriptions with graceful scrollwork, monograms, coats of arms and other simple features (plates 1 and 2). The blanks are beautifully designed in traditional or modern style by himself and made at Powell's, where he is the chief designer and managing director. Laurence Whistler, whose work is of the highest class, depicts mainly pictorial and decorative subjects, often very closely associated with his poetry. It must be mentioned that Laurence Whistler began his revival of diamond-point work quite independently of, and at about the same time as, W. J. Wilson. Both artists were entirely self-taught. The difference between the types of subject matter and also the styles of W. J. Wilson and Laurence Whistler may be clearly seen from the illustrations of their work.

Today, diamond-point work is also done by about half a dozen other engravers, whose work is illustrated in this book. Often these craftsmen are not solely glass engravers by profession, but free-lance artist craftsmen. They have evolved their own particular versions of the technique, and many are self-taught. All produce commemorative pieces as well as pictorial and purely decorative work for patrons and the public market. These craftsmen normally buy their blanks individually, or in sets, from wholesalers and retailers and they are not, therefore, designed especially for them, while for certain commissioned work they, and others, may have glasses made to their own designs or work in collaboration with designers in the glassmaking industry. Laurence Whistler worked on antique glasses for many years as he believed their metal, craftsmanship and shape to be superior to that obtainable at the time, but for the past five years or so he has seldom used antique glass, as he now has goblets, wineglasses, panels, etc., made to his own design by Whitefriars.

Only very occasionally today do glass manufacturers produce diamond-point work. The craft was revived by some manufacturers, however, to produce commemorative pieces for the Coronation of Queen Elizabeth II.

Wheel engraving today is done both in the industry (illustrated in plates 4, 5, 6, 7, 8 and 9) and by free-lance craftsmen. There is at the moment a Department of Glass Design at the Edinburgh College of Art, where wheel engravers and other artists in glass decoration are trained under the direction of Helen Monro, who, as perhaps the foremost wheel engraver of today, has led a revival of the craft in this country. Miss Monro trained on the Continent and in this country. The Foley College of Further Education and School of Art, Stourbridge, is training apprentices for the local industry. The Royal College of Art and other Colleges of Art have Departments of Industrial Glass. A few glasshouses which produce handmade blown table glassware have wheel engravers on the staff of their decoration shops. Often the designs on the industrially decorated glass are rather formalised and sometimes tend to become lifeless as the engraver becomes too familiar with the design after constant repetition (plate 5). Individual pieces of engraved glass are still produced at these glasshouses on special occasions (plates 8 and 9). The designs and craftsmanship of wheel-engraved glass produced by free-lance engravers are usually alive, spontaneous and beautifully executed. Helen Monro, Harold Gordon and Dorothy Brown were trained as wheel engravers and it is believed have at some time worked in industry, but all are now independent craftsmen. John Hutton, Stephen Rickard and David Peace cannot technically be termed wheel engravers as they use wheels and abrasive tools in a hand chuck (plate 10). David Peace, like some others, combines both forms of engraving on the same piece and in the same design with great success. The serifs of his lettering are usually done with the diamond- or steel-point, while the body of the letters is executed with his wheels. It is practically impossible to decide where the one method stops and the other begins. Miss E. J. Webster has found that she has not been able to depict satisfactorily certain textures such as hair, by wheel engraving. In an attempt to overcome this problem Miss Webster first tried to use the diamond-point on the untouched glass surface, and again the result was disappointing because of the loss of modelling in form, although texture was achieved (plate 11). Now, by a combination of wheel and diamond techniques, she has produced successful results. Her method is to engrave *and* polish out the form of the area, to produce the modelling, and then apply the drawing with a diamond-point, to produce the texture (as seen in plate 12, the bee).

Again, the blanks used by these craftsmen are bought individually from wholesalers or retailers, the blanks used by both types of engravers being of English, Swedish or Dutch metal and craftsmanship, and also those made to their own specifications by English and foreign glasshouses; the individual craftsman selects the shapes and types of metal most suited to his technique, and in addition chooses perfect or near perfect craftsmanship, colour and tone of blank when struck.

In other countries work of a parallel nature is carried on by artists working either independently or for glassworks. On the continent perhaps the most famous of modern diamond-point engravers was the late Gertrude Bohnert, a Swiss, whose delicate flower studies and animal subjects are illustrated in plates 66, 67 and 68. Her style was characteristic of the folk artists of her country. The diamond-point engraving by W. Heesen on the crystal dish shown in plate 69 is typically Dutch and the subject matter is traditional. Mr. Heesen was responsible for the modern revival of diamond-point engraving in Holland, the country of its former highest expression. In distinct contrast with the Swiss and Dutch work is the modern Italian diamond-point work illustrated in plate 70.

As in this country, so elsewhere, is engraving by wheel more widely practised than by diamond-point. In Copenhagen an independent artist, Åse Voss Schrader, is now producing some very fine work; an example is to be seen in plate 32. Also in Denmark were produced the four glasses illustrated in plate 31. The wheel engraving was done between 1934 and 1940 at Holmegaards Glasvaerk by Elving Runemalm, a Swedish craftsman, to the designs of Jacob E. Bang, who is now with the Kastrup Glasvaerk.

"A new conception of the material as a 'frozen liquid' decoration with lavishly engraved patterns, and a standard of excellence in design which is expressed in the most humble utilitarian object as well as the most sophisticated luxury wares, has made the new *Scandinavian glass tradition* one of the dominant factors of the contemporary scene."

There has been a great movement toward quantity production of small decorated vases and the like by even the most famous glassworks such as Orrefors and Kosta. Naturally the popularisation of the craft of wheel engraving has led to an increased demand for semi-mass-produced work which has resulted in the lack of feeling expressed in much of the engraving. Nevertheless, the work on the more expensive and unique pieces is quite superb. This is to be seen from the photographs, plates 28, 73, 74 and 76. Simon Gate and Edward Hald were largely responsible, through Orrefors, for the revival in Swedish glassmaking. They both placed very great emphasis on design. Vicke Lindstrand is now with Kosta Glasvaerk. Quite distinct from the now accepted modern traditional Scandinavian style in design is the work done in Finland at the Karhula-Iittala Glassworks. The plates 29 and 42 show work produced some years ago, but they are included for reasons stated elsewhere in the text.

In the United States, Steuben Glass has been responsible for outstanding work. Not only has it effectively developed the production of fine glass and fine wheel engraving by its own designers, glassmakers and wheel engravers, illustrated in plates 14, 15 and 75, but it has also undertaken two most interesting and challenging projects. The outcome of these projects are the collections 'British Artists in Crystal' and 'Asian Artists in Crystal' which are represented in part in plates 16, 17, 18, 58, and 19, 20, 21 and 22 respectively. The works are the result of collaboration between the various artists who devised the designs to be transcribed to glass, and the designers, glassmakers and engravers of Steuben Glass where the complete finalisation took place. In the first place the British and Asian artists independently created the designs, and it is particularly noticeable that in the vast majority of cases these are traditionally religious, racial, national and geographical, that is, for example, the Oriental artists were not influenced by Western subjects or techniques when devising their designs. The Steuben designers worked out the most suitable shapes to carry the designs, and blanks were made to their drawings. The designs were then transferred onto these blanks by copper-wheel engraving. It is especially noteworthy that the engravers have achieved remarkable success in conveying the essential feeling of each design. 'Calligraphy, a venerated art to the Chinese, is an exacting expression of the artist's ability.' If this is held to be true then the artistic ability of the engraver is superb.

CHAPTER TWO

DESIGNING A PIECE OF GLASS AND ITS DECORATION

THE DESIRE to create beauty is instinctive to mankind. Glass is a medium through which the artist and craftsman are able to express themselves, usually in a utilitarian manner. However, graphic artists of high repute in their own line often fail when they attempt to transfer their talent to designing the shape of a glass blank, or the decoration for a glass blank. They cannot overcome the obstacle that they know little about at first hand, of this very difficult medium. It has been said that it is only when a man has handled molten glass for many years, and has acquired a fair degree of mastery over it, that he knows its capabilities and limitations. It is extremely rare for one man to handle the glass throughout its production from conception to completion, and there are many designers and decorators of glass who have successfully, and often brilliantly, captured the understanding of the material without practical experience of glassmaking.

Every glass is the outcome of design. Design may come about in three ways: (a) by original inspiration, (b) by modification for use, and (c) by modification for manufacture. Whether using one or other of these ways it is most undesirable that the designer of the blank should go beyond the means of his material, to try to make it do something for which it is not naturally capable.

In industry it is usual to conceive the piece of glass in its entirety: that is, either as a piece of glass complete in itself, or as a decorated piece of glass. In the latter case the industrial, or the artist-craftsman designer of the whole piece must decide upon the decorative motif to be applied, and the method by which that decoration is to be reproduced on or in the surface of the blank. The qualities of the decorative motif itself control the shape of the blank, for it should be complementary to the form (both in elevation and the round), nature and character of the glass. The shape of the glass and the decorative motif it carries are ideally complementary in the *Merry-Go-Round Bowl*, plate 14. In addition to this the processes and techniques involved in applying the decoration must be considered for they will govern to some extent the shape of the blank. Practically all the tools employed in each of the decorative processes impose limitations of one form or another. When the designer of a glass blank intends that it shall be decorated by the removal of glass by some method, he must consider the thickness of the glass about the area to be decorated. Generally, there seems to be no rule that certain thicknesses of glass are required for the individual decorative processes, or that certain decorative processes can be applied only to specific thicknesses of glass. Nevertheless, it is often the case that on a thick-walled glass it seems obviously incorrect to have a shallow decoration, where only the very surface of the glass has been removed, by acid etching and wheel engraving, or decoration of a slight character, exampled in open motifs executed with the diamond-point. If the depth of glass at the intended area of decoration is thin, then the degree to which modelling of form may be taken is decreased, and bold modelling is impossible.

One example where the method of applying the decoration governs the shape of the specially made, or specially selected, blank is where 'wheel engraving' is executed by means of a hand-chuck method. Those decorators who use this method often find it difficult to obtain good results on concave surfaces.

Those etchers and engravers who buy their blanks from retail shops have the responsibility of choosing those which are most suited to their own particular method of decoration, and also suited to bear the decorative motif which they wish to apply. On the other hand, often the very shape of an undecorated blank prompts the motif which the decorator applies to it. Possibly the first responsibility is the most important, for often a motif is not so very rigid in form that it cannot be altered slightly to enable it to be complementary to the shape of the blank.

DECORATIVE PROCESSES

THE PROCESSES and techniques involved in carrying out the application of the motif must be remembered when designing the form of the blank. These applied decorative processes may be categorised as follows :—

(a) *Decoration with the aid of heat*: — Hand and machine blowing and shaping; applied ornament in the form of trailing, rigoree, prunts, claws, etc.; flashing; double dipping; enamelling; staining; pressing.

(b) *Decoration by chemical action*: — Clear acid embossing; deep acid, or 'rotting'; white acid etching; satin acid etching; French, or triple embossing; fluoride pastes.

(c) *Decoration by abrasion*: — Cutting; intaglio; wheel engraving; diamond-point engraving; sand-blasting.

(d) *Decoration by adhesives*: — Painting and transferring, where the permanency is obtained by heating or 'firing.'

There is no reason, as far as I am aware, why any two or more of the above-mentioned methods of decoration, with their different characteristics, may not be used together to very good effect, on one piece of glass. Very interesting effects may be obtained if a pattern is engraved, sandblasted or etched through the coloured metal of a piece of flashed glass. Another example is when a plant motif is built up of polished and unpolished cut leaves on an acid etched or sand blasted stem.

THE QUALITIES OF GLASS

I WILL TAKE some of the qualities of glass and analyse them to show how they must be respected by the designer and decorator of the blank, if the best results are to be obtained.

The clear transparency of glass. In the case of glassware one side of the article must agree rhythmically with the other side. Viewed from any angle one sees through the near side of the glass. When one studies a glass one's eyes focus on one side or surface of it, but when normally one glances at a glass shape, one's eyes, by very quick alteration of focal length, see both surfaces or sides of the glass with nearly equal clarity. The object should not always have to be studied for its beauty to become apparent. This means that the near side should normally be designed in relation to the far side, and the decoration upon or cut into it must also bear a relation to the far side (plates 24, 25, and 56). The work of David Peace provides us with interesting illustrations by a craftsman who has realised these qualities. As in all engraving, the work is carried out on the external surface of the glass. In the *Lavabo Bowl* (plate 24) the inscriptions have added meaning because, when in use, the declaration and response are completely visible to those who perform the ceremony. Both inscriptions are engraved in reverse on the farther rim. In plate 25 the owner of the goblet, the Archbishop of York, is easily reminded of its origin *as he uses it,* for the inscription is so positioned and engraved in reverse on the farther rim of the goblet that it may be read in entirety from the front. In these two examples we see that the artist has been careful to work out the shape of the area on the bowls of the glasses that can be clearly seen *when they are in use,* and to so arrange his lettering that it conforms to that shape. The front of the goblet (plate 25) provides an excellent example of the relationship which the engraver has achieved between the shape of the elevation of the bowl, and the shape of the decorative motif, the shield, etc. This 'space-filling' adds definition to the shape of the goblet's bowl.

Aquatic subjects are complementary to the transparent and liquid nature of glass. This is to be noted in plates 8, 27, 28 and 66.

Glass is a liquid. In the molten state glass is viscous. Glass is shown off at its best when this liquid, viscous, plastic, sluggish nature of the metal is expressed and retained in a shape of great beauty. A glass vessel is first blown as a bubble of glass and the less its appearance as a bubble is disturbed the better (plate 20). Hard angles and corners in a blown shape are best avoided as are many forms not natural to its manipulation as a bubble. This does not apply to pressed glass because corners are natural to the mould. Glass is a congealed super-cooled liquid; it is like pottery in that it is fashioned from a malleable material, but unlike pottery in that it is plastic only in the molten condition and sets on cooling. This temporary property of plasticity enables it to be fashioned. The designer of the blank must realise the speed at which the craftsmen have to work because plasticity is only temporary. The 'bubble' form of most glassware generally controls the nature of the motif. Often the most suitable motif is one which incorporates round forms as these are complementary to the 'bubble.' Lettering, which is often composed of straight lines may, however, be a very effective form of decoration. The lettering seen in plate 33 is intended primarily as pure decoration and the significance of the letters is of slightly less importance. The letters define the straight form of the elevation of the glass. In plate 34 the letters are of a rounded or oval style, and again define the shape of the decanter, in this case of a more oval elevation.

As a material glass in the cool state is hard and durable. This naturally implies that any decoration must be permanent. Because of this, sandblasting, etching, engraving, cutting and enamelling are more satisfactory than cold adhesives and transfers. Enamelling and painting take upon themselves the surface appearance of the glass itself and therefore look correct. The removal of glass as a form of decoration demands a high degree of skill and accuracy on the part of the etcher or engraver, for any mistakes cannot be rectified once the surface of the glass has been removed.

Glass is relatively soft in the cool state. By this oxymoron with the previous paragraph I imply that it is relatively easy to take away the surface of the glass either by abrasion or chemical action. This quality has enabled many decorative techniques to be developed. This and the preceding quality must be considered if the designer of the blank wishes a decoration to be reproduced upon or in the shape. The shape must not be too clumsy to handle while the particular decorative processes are being carried out.

Glass is a cheap material to manufacture. This puts a moral responsibility on the designer, as glass is in daily use in the millions of homes all over the world. This means that every glass article made should have that essential rightness for its job and be a thing of beauty, too, whatever its function. A beautiful object is usually as cheap as, and often cheaper than, an ugly one—to produce. The insistence upon good design in every article made will ensure the survival of the glass industry in competition with more recent industries, such as plastics.

Glass is easily cracked and broken. The walls of a vessel should be reasonably consistent in thickness and the change from thick to thin walls gradual. Thick and thin walls in juxtaposition will result in cracking on sudden change in temperature, unless carefully annealed after the forming of the vessel. Handles, knobs, feet, etc., must be designed not to be a nuisance under a normal amount of handling.

Glass is capable of great beauty, often, if left alone. Decoration can spoil the inherent beauty of even a simple glass shape. This is a responsibility for the decorator of glass. The basic shape of glasses can be varied safely only within comparatively narrow limits. Technically clever results may be obtained, but they may nevertheless offend the aesthetic sense. Decoration, however, can be varied almost endlessly, and numerous different designs can be applied to the same shape. Graphic or pictorial art, if handled with discretion, lends itself to the decoration of the surface of the shape.

In a wide sense good shape and inherent or self-colour constitute decorative elements. Glass lends itself readily to very varied decoration. Until recently the greater proportion of decoration could have been left off glass to its very definite advantage. It is generally quite wrong to cover a shape with cutting or engraving as it destroys its plastic appearance and the glass ceases to look like a bubble. Often there should be only sufficient decoration to enhance the other qualities of the glass. The decoration must be in keeping with, and complementary to, the design of the shape.

It is common practice to put an imitation cut glass design on an obviously pressed glass article, while the article is in the mould. This is an anachronism dating from the time when cut glass was expensive to produce; and there is no reason for it today, when cut glass is reasonably cheap and the imitation fails to deceive the buying public. The surface texture of pressed glass has a beauty of its own and the decoration of pressed glass should be developed along its own lines, the only limitations being those imposed by the mould itself, such as quick release, or decoration to obscure the seams of a hinged mould.

Glass is light catching and has great powers of reflections and refraction. The responsiveness of the surface to light results in the changing play of light that can give added life to a design. This perhaps is the magic of the material. The ability of glass to refract light and to break it down into the colours of the spectrum has been made much of; this is shown by the popularity of cut glass. It has been a popular form of decoration since the latter half of the eighteenth century to cut glass into facets to obtain as a result a mass of sparkling colour. However, this really wonderful quality of glass has led to a stagnation of design in cut glass. As a style of decoration it is much too limited in scope. The cuts and facets apart from the production of the spectrum colours are all too often meaningless in themselves and uninspired in their arrangement. This style of design has dominated glass decoration in this country for the last 150 years, becoming more dull and stereotyped year by year. Very recently there has been a reaction against it; there is now a trend to produce articles on which cutting has been used in the barest minimum.

These are some of the qualities and peculiarities of glass : the qualities that have to be respected and turned to good account by the designer of the blank, and also the decorator who uses it.

CHAPTER THREE

MAKING A HANDMADE BLOWN GLASS VESSEL

THE MAKING OF THE METAL

GLASS IS A hard non-crystalline, transparent or opaque vitreous substance which is the result of the fusion of silica, or the best pure white sand, with active mineral solvents or fluxes.

There are numerous types of glass, each used for different purposes, and each for different reasons. Handmade glassware is practically always made with either full-crystal or demi-crystal metal; pressed glassware is nearly always made of soda-lime metal; while oven-ware or heat-resisting glassware is made of a boro-silicate metal.

The formulae for these types of metal obviously vary, and obviously, too, they have different ingredients. Apart from these differences there is also a difference between the formulae for the same type of metal between one glasshouse and another. Each manufacturer slightly increases, or decreases, the amount of the constituents, or perhaps adds a small quantity of something else, which, although insignificantly, does change the basic formulae. Each manufacturer believes his formulae to be the best and naturally keeps the formulae a secret.

However, the basic formulae are known, and are as follows :—

Full-lead crystal

Sand	50%
Red lead	32.5%
Potassium carbonate	17.5%

also saltpetre and decolourisers, to which, when molten, is added a quantity of cullet (see Glossary) equal to half the quantity of the molten batch.

Full-crystal glass has not less than 30 per cent. lead and demi-crystal or half-crystal 15 per cent. lead. When the sand, potash and lead oxide are heated together at a high temperature, usually between 1,300 degrees and 1,500 degrees centigrade, the sand is dissolved by the solvent action of the fused potash and lead. This process takes approximately 36 hours. The brilliancy and density of the glass is due to the lead oxide, the transparency and hardness to the sand, the purity of colour and translucency to the potash, the strength, toughness and elasticity of the glass to the method by which it is made. The property of transparency is not one that might be expected from the appearance of the constituents of the glass.

The sand is purified by washing, and then drying by flame while in the process of being sieved. Silver sand is obtained from a mine at Loch Aline, or from quarries at King's Lynn and Redhill. Some sand is imported from Fontainebleau, France; Limburg, Holland; and the Campine, Belgium.

The red lead is a derivative of metallic lead, and as stated above contributes to the diamond-like brilliancy. Red lead is imported from Australia.

The potassium carbonate helps to obtain brilliancy also, as well as giving reflective power and freedom from colour. It is interesting to note that when a glassmaker says that the metal 'has a good colour' he usually means that it is free from all colour.

The cullet has to be of the same chemical composition as that to which it will be added, i.e. full-lead crystal cullet for full-lead crystal metal and not full-lead crystal cullet for a soda-lime metal, or vice versa. The cullet is usually obtained from the firm's own rejects and breakages, or from a known outside source. Decolourisers, or glass-maker's soap, are usually a salt of arsenic or oxide of manganese. The metal is always decolourised, even if it is intended that it should have a definite colour when produced. The colours are added only to a clear transparent metal.

Colourisers. The colour is put into the metal by adding certain metallic oxides to the batch. A certain selection of examples are :—

Colour	Oxide
Blue	Cobalt or Copper
Purple	Nickel or Manganese
Brown	Manganese or Iron
Red (Ruby)	Gold, Selenium or Copper
Amber	Selenium, or Carbon plus Sulphur
Green	Iron, Copper or Chromium

Soda-lime metal

Sand	70%
Soda ash	18%
Lime	12%

The lime acts as a flux. The stone is quarried in Derbyshire.

The soda is manufactured in Cheshire from salt. Sodium carbonate is used, but potassium ensures more brilliance.

Boro-silicate metal. Boro-silicate metal contains 12% boric acid and up to 80% sand which gives the property of limiting expansion (i.e. it lowers the coefficient of expansion of metal).

The batch is melted in a fire-clay crucible or pot varying in capacity from $\frac{1}{4}$ cwt. up to two tons. Pot furnaces, according to the size of the furnace and also the capacity of the pots, house from six to twenty pots at a time. A tank-furnace holds up to 1,000 tons of metal, and is used in sheet or plate glassworks.

The central feature of a glasshouse, the pot furnace, is built of refractory brick and steel, and is fired by coke, oil and sometimes gas, the flues of the furnace passing out between the pot positions. The pots are placed around the circumference of the furnace, their apertures directed outward. This is usually the only part of the furnace which is seen, as the 'shop' floors are built up to the height of the pots for easy, quick working.

THE MAKING OF THE BLOWN VESSEL

BLOWING IS THE traditional method of making glassware. It is still widely used although the automatic machinery which has been derived from the traditional hand method is lessening the demand on glass-blowers.

The tools of the glassblower are relatively primitive in character. There has been very little change in their design or purpose since their conception. This is due to the fact that the processes and techniques involved in glassblowing were evolved very early in the story of glassmaking and have not been and cannot be improved upon.

Glassblowers work in teams of four : the workman (chairman or gaffer), the servitor, the footmaker, and boy or taker-in (who takes the finished articles to the lehr), in that order of seniority. The footmaker is the apprentice, the servitor is a craftsman and the workman a master-craftsman of some twenty years' experience.

A bowl or dish. The footmaker dips his blow-iron into the metal, or molten batch, and gathers, by touch and eye only, the correct amount of metal required for the shape or blank. This metal has to be bubble free. The footmaker then marvers the gather on the marver, an unheated polished iron slab, in order to make it, symmetrical, of the desired shape, and in the desired position relative to the iron. The

30

next operation the footmaker undertakes is to blow the gather into shape. This is done by blowing down the iron tube while holding the mouthpiece to the lips (plate 35). The metal then forms a bubble, whose shape is regulated by the position in which the iron is held. If the iron is held upward the bulb, or bubble, becomes spherical; downward the bulb becomes elongated and pear-shaped. When the iron is moved in a circular fashion at head height the bulb becomes cylindrical.

The servitor here takes over, and sitting in the chair rotates the blow-iron, and of course, metal, by rolling the tube on the two long straight arms of the chair. This rolling is carried out with the left hand (assuming he is right-handed), while with the right the servitor is manipulating the glass into the desired shape by means of willow wood armed spring pincers and a pearwood pat, bat or board, similar to a butterpat (plate 36).

Willow and pearwood are used because when charred they produce a fine non-abrasive, and even lubricating, charcoal. These wooden tools are frequently dipped into water during the shaping of the molten glass. Gradually they burn away and wear out and have to be replaced.

A solid rod, or punty, is attached to the metal next, by means of a molten blob of glass. Molten glass readily welds itself to a more solid material. This connection is made at the centre of the bottom, underside of the future bowl, directly opposite the blow-iron, and on the same axis. The blow-iron is detached by cooling the glass at the end of the blow-iron by pouring water on it, and then giving the hardened glass a sharp tap with a convenient tool, so fracturing the iron from the glass.

The process is now continued by the workman, who either finally shapes the bowl by opening out the bulb by means of his willow wood pincers or by shearing off the excess glass with a pair of large specially made scissors (plate 37). The metal during these processes, even though they are necessarily conducted at relatively high speed, becomes too stiff to manipulate easily. It is therefore necessary to reheat the metal so that it again becomes workable. The reheating, termed warming-in, is done in the 'glory-hole,' a small subsidiary furnace. When the final desired shape is obtained the metal is allowed to harden by cooling, and is detached from the punty by the application of a sharp tap to the necessary part of the joint.

The bowl is now annealed in a lehr, where, by reheating and very gradual cooling to normal handling temperature, the stress and strain created within the glass during shaping is removed. Lack of annealing would cause the glass bowl to shatter with a loud report, like a Prince Rupert Drop, if knocked even gently.

After annealing, the process of puntying is undertaken. This process is the removal, by grinding, of the glass blob by which the punty is attached to the bowl. This is the final process, and apart from any applied decoration to be carried out at the designer's wish, the bowl is complete. Decoration, such as colouring and shaping of the bowl, may be carried out in the actual manufacture.

A stemmed and footed piece. The same processes and techniques are employed as for making a bowl until the stage is reached where the punty is attached to the bowl. This process is **not** carried out; instead a blob of glass is attached to the bottom of the bowl and then drawn out to the desired length; this forms the stem. A second, smaller, bulb is now 'welded' to the stem and detached from its separate punty. This bulb is now opened out with the aid of the various tools at the glassblower's disposal.

The wineglass is now complete except for completing the wineglass bowl. This is undertaken by clasping the newly formed foot in a special tool called a gadget. The blow-iron is detached from the bowl in the manner described before. The bowl can now be modelled to the desired shape by the workman. This is a stuck stem glass. Straw-stemmed glasses are made by drawing the metal, at the bottom of the bowl, into a stem and then adding a foot.

Handled glassware. Handles are added to the completed shape while it is still on the punty. A molten bar of metal is pressed to the side of the bowl and then bent round to the required shape and attached to the bowl again. The lower joint of the handle is undertaken first. The metal for the handle is manipulated with a pair of pincers or tongs.

Every piece of glassware has to be annealed after making for the reasons given above. In the modern 'shops' puntying is always undertaken. Many artist-craftsmen engravers engrave their names on the ground punty position.

CHAPTER FOUR

ETCHING GLASS

THE PROCESSES and techniques set out below are those normally under-taken by artist-craftsmen in order to produce individual pieces of decorated glass, such as those illustrated in plates 38, 39, 40 and 50. These methods may be adapted to quantity production, and with little additional planning work such as in illustrations in plates 41 and 48 may be produced.

The etching of glass, known to the trade as 'embossing,' is a process whereby glass is obscured by dissolving its surface by some solution containing hydrofluoric acid, the only acid that will rapidly attack glass. By etching, an almost infinite variety of obscuring textures can be obtained and these in combination are capable of extremely interest-ing decorative effects.

There are several standard finishes that are employed for their decorative appearance as well as for their obscuring or concealing qualities. In this book, however, I am primarily concerned with the decoration by etching.

ACID FINISHES FOR GLASSWARE

ACID TREATMENT can conveniently be divided into two types; clear and white. Solutions of hydrofluoric acid, usually called clear acid, dissolve the glass but leave the surface comparatively clear. The addition, however, of a strong neutralising alkali produces a frosted obscured surface, and the combination of hydrofluoric acid and alkali (usually sodium or ammonium bifluoride) is known as white acid from which the finish derives its name.

If the white acid tone on a glass is treated with dilute hydrofluoric acid, the frosted surface effect becomes more clear by being partially dissolved away, leaving a satin finish. This satin finish may be varied in tone by the time of treatment or the strength of the acid, and tones in combination on the same piece may be obtained by protecting the glass with acid-resisting materials at various stages of the acid biting.

A summary of acid finishes for glassware is as follows :—

Clear acid	*White acid*
(hydrofluoric)	(hydrofluoric + a bifluoride)
Clear etch	Satin etch
Deep etch	French embossing
Rotting	

PREPARING THE BLANK FOR SINGLE-TONE ETCHING

THE GLASS VESSEL, of whatever nature or shape, is first wiped dry and clean, and then given a thin even overall coating of Brunswick Black, or Embossing Black, as it is called. The Brunswick Black is resistant against the acid and is a sufficient protection for a limited time. An added protection is given, which also provides a suitable stencil material for the cutting of the design; this is a coating of a thin lead foil which is now applied. A foil of 0.002″ in thickness is suitable. The foil is first checked for any pinholes or tears through which the acid is able to pass. The blackened glass and one side of the foil are then given a thin even coating of a soft beeswax-tallow mixture. The beeswax is yet another acid resist, but its main purpose is to act as an adhesive between the foil and blackened glass. The consistency of the soft wax is rather critical; too soft and the foil will slip and move on the glass; too hard, and the foil will not peel away easily later. The problem of covering the round form is overcome by cutting the foil into suitably shaped pieces and applying them piece by piece, overlapping the foil panels where necessary. The entire surface of the shape should be covered with the foil as the shape is to be submerged in the acid. The foil is pasted or rubbed down to the glass surface evenly so that it presents a smooth even surface, free from lumps and air bubbles. The glass vessel is now ready for the application of the design tracing.

The tracing, in black pencil or ink on light tissue, is attached to the foil by means of the beeswax mixture. The etching on a glass vessel takes place on the outside, so the tracing is not reversed, as normally the outer surfaces are workable. It is sometimes difficult to apply a flat tracing to a curved glass surface. Two methods are used to overcome this problem. The first is by cutting the tracing into sections that can be stuck round the shape in mosaic fashion; and the second is to apply a thin coating of a mixture of whiting and gum arabic, which when dry will provide a surface upon which a pencil drawing can easily be made.

The design having been transferred to the shape by any of the above three methods, the stencil is now cut; for this a sharp thin-bladed knife or scalpel is used. All the lines of the design are now cut and the tracing and foil peeled off the areas where the etching is to take place. For a single tone etching these pieces are discarded, but for a dual or multitone etching they must be retained. With the foil now removed, the Brunswick Black is revealed.

It may be found that the edges of the foil may be burred or lifted due either to a blunted knife or incorrect cutting. These edges should be burnished quite flat with a bone burnishing tool or the back of an old spoon. The firmer the foil is burnished down to the glass, the easier will be the subsequent removal of the Brunswick Black, and the safer the foil against the encroachment of acid under the edges during etching, with the resultant indistinct outline of the design. All exposed areas of Brunswick Black must now be cleaned, as indeed must any surplus tracing or wax on the remaining foil. If any wax is left on the foil there will be the great tendency of the bristles of the brush to smear the wax across the clear glass etching areas. The result is a streaky, patchy etch and a very dirty acid brush. Cleanliness of laboratory standards should be aimed for at all stages of acid embossing. A soft rag damped but not saturated in turpentine is used to remove the Black and remaining traces of wax and paper. It is essential that the whole article should finally possess only clean bright areas of foil and clear exposed areas of glass where etching is to take place. The shape is now ready for etching.

ETCHING THE BLANK

THE ETCHING OF the blank is carried out by submerging the shape in a tank of the appropriate acid, for the required finish, for the correct length of time. The length of time depends upon the depth of design required and also the thickness of the glass. If possible, a trial is made on a spare piece of the same glass, to determine the time. Different types of glass and different strengths of acids etch at varying rates. The tank containing acid is usually of lead, and always of acid-resisting material. The size, shape and thickness of wall of the tank depends upon the size and shape of the blank. The recent introduction of polythene provides reasonably cheap containers in the form of household bowls and pails.

For a Clear Etch

> Hydrofluoric acid (full strength)   1 part
> to Water   3 parts

is used, the shape being submerged from fifteen minutes to several hours according to the depth of etch required. If a smooth, very clear etch is required four or more parts of water are added to one part of acid and the surface of the glass is brushed with a soft hair brush, or alternatively a polythene pastry brush, in order to keep the acid solution and sediment in circulation.

For a Clear Deep Etch

> Hydrofluoric acid (full strength)   1 part
> to Water   2 or 3 parts

is used; the design area being brushed constantly and the acid restrengthened every half-hour. The sediment is washed from the design during restrengthening of the acid.

For 'Rotting'

> Hydrofluoric acid (full strength)   1 part
> to Water   2 or 3 parts

is used. 'Rotting' is best obtained by allowing the undissolved glass deposits to fall away unevenly from the glass surface. This is purely a 'chance' process with unguaranteed and sometimes unexpected results. Things, however, can be **influenced** but not definitely controlled by either (a) the lime content of the glass or (b) the angle the glass surface presents to the acid. In the horizontal or face-up position for say a dish or bowl, the results may be disappointing, for the glass deposits are not able to fall away in this position. Certainly, due to the interference of these deposits, the etching process will be slow. In a near vertical position the deposits will fall away more readily, except on the edges of the foil, thus giving quicker and more reliable results. In the inverted position with the areas of etching face down in the acid, rotting takes place quickly and with good results. In these two latter positions care must be taken that small air bubbles do not cling to or form on the glass etching surface. To overcome this the glass article should be gently tapped or shaken in the acid to release the air bubbles. Acid rotting is quite a chancy procedure, especially with some type of glasses, and the results can range from the successful, as exampled in plate 42, to the disappointing. The acid and sediment are not disturbed in any way during the process. The etching time is according to requirements.

For a White Matt Etch. White acid as supplied by trade producers is used; trade products are used according to the manufacturers' specifications, and are never strengthened or diluted. When the acid becomes 'tired' and dirty it is thrown away and fresh acid is used. Etching time is usually fifteen minutes to half an hour. The design is not brushed, and a white deposit is left on the surface of the glass when etching is complete; this is removed by washing in tap water.

White acid is easily affected by patches of grease or fingerprints on the glass surface, and a patchy etch may result. To overcome this the glass article may be pre-washed in a bath of one part hydrofluoric acid to three or four parts of water, for a period of three or four minutes. This will help to remove any slight grease patches and also remove the 'skin' of the glass which will present a new surface for the white acid to work on.

For a satin Etch. First the design is white matt etched for about fifteen minutes. The shape is removed from the white acid tank, washed and placed in clear etch acid for ten minutes or more according to requirements. A large range of satin tones are possible by varying the clear etch time.

FRENCH EMBOSSING OR MULTI-TONE ETCHING

THE SHAPE IS prepared as for a single-tone etch, and the design cut, burnished and cleaned. The largest area is now etched and when the required tone is reached the glass is removed from the bath, washed and dried. The next process is that of partially remasking the design by blacking and replacing the necessary area of cut away foil. This is done carefully to prevent tears and gaps being made through which acid may pass. The design is again prepared for etching, making sure that the foil is burnished and surplus wax removed, and this process carried out. These processes are repeated until the design is complete, the largest area being etched first, and the design area being blocked in as required while other etching processes are undertaken, until at the final etch the smallest area is exposed. The shape is washed and cleaned as before.

POST ETCHING PROCESSES

WHEN ETCHING IS complete the acids are allowed to stand for some time to let the dirt settle. The clean, good acid is poured off and and retained for future use. The dirt is thrown away. In all cases except white acid, the strength of the acids after usage is regained by adding full strength acid. White acid is not usually diluted or strengthened and is used only for a limited period before discarding.

The etched glass is first washed clean with tap water, and then the foil is stripped off. The Brunswick Black is cleaned off with a rag wet with turpentine and then with sawdust. The glass is finally cleaned with warm water and soap.

The etched surfaces are now clearly readable with clear sharply defined edges.

MASS PRODUCTION OF DESIGNS BY ACID ETCHING

FOR THE MASS production of designs on glass any of the accepted methods of silk-screening are used. The acid resist is made up of Brunswick Black stiffened up to the correct consistency for printing by the addition of French chalk which acts as a drier, and is acid resistant in itself, it being made of finely ground mica. The design to be printed is stopped out on the silk by being printed with varnish, cut out of 'Profilm' and being ironed into it or made photographically on 'Photostencil' paper.

Messrs. Stevens & Williams Ltd. use a method whereby the design is first cut in the positive on a block (plate 43) then copper-plated. The design is printed on a paper 'stencil' using acid-resist ink, and the design then transferred, before the ink dries, to the glass vessel (plates 44 and 45). This leaves the clean areas of the glass surface to be attacked by the acid; according to the design, other areas are 'blacked' in by brush before dipping into the acid bath (plates 46 and 47). The finished article is shown in plate 48.

Acid badging is a method similar in some ways to the one just described but the idea of the stencil is reversed. A copper plate is engraved in the positive, and a smooth fluoride paste is then applied and the surplus removed. The recesses in the engraved plate are thus charged with acid paste. Special tissue paper is next applied to the plate, and is printed with a thin film of acid paste in the desired design form. The charged paper is then applied to the glass for a few moments to allow the action between acid and glass to take place.

Many firms employ the method whereby the shape, to provide it with a decorative layer, is dipped into molten acid-resistant wax. The wax is allowed to solidify so that the design may be drawn on to its surface. The unwanted areas of wax are then removed by means of small scrapers, after which the article is etched in the manner already described. Plate 49 shows the transference of the design to the waxed shape of an individual piece, the completed form of which is shown in plate 50. The whole process may be done automatically and at relatively high speed when the articles are of a suitable shape and the designs are of a regular nature. The design is not drawn on to the wax, but a mechanically operated stylus scribes away the unwanted solidified wax. The patterns produced are usually of line form and are reproduced by the pantograph method. The main designs are of the Grecian key, ribbon and interlocking or running circle type.

THE ACID TREATMENT OF FLASHED GLASSES

ONE OF THE oldest applications of the use of acid in glass decoration is the removal of the flashing of a coloured glass from another clear base glass. The thin skin of coloured glass can be removed by dilute clear acid, either completely (leaving a pattern of coloured glass on a clear background) or vice versa (a clear pattern on a coloured background) as seen in plate 38; or else the flashing can be removed in stages, the acid being timed to give any tone from the pure colour to clear glass, as shown in plate 39.

CHAPTER FIVE

ENGRAVING GLASS BY DIAMOND POINT

DIAMOND-POINT ENGRAVING is executed entirely by hand, using a small diamond, set in a holder similar to a penholder or pencil (plate 51). Some artists, however, prefer to use a tungsten carbide tipped steel 'pencil.' More will be said later concerning the advantages and disadvantages of both tools. Until then, and thereafter, the technique will be referred to as diamond point.

The artist uses the diamond point either to scratch the surface of the glass, drawing the design as with a pencil in line (plate 66); or to stipple it (plates 52, 53, 54, 57 and 59), which is a similar work of a more delicate nature carried out in dots or in very fine short lines. In the latter case it approaches the first style. Usually both styles are combined to achieve the desired result.

The shape of the actual diamond of the diamond-point 'pencil' is a four or six-sided pyramid. Its base is set in metal at one end of a pencil or pen-shaped plastic or wooden holder-handle. The scribing action employed when 'drawing' on the surface of the glass enables the point of the diamond pyramid to dig into and scratch the glass. In fact, the scratch is a series of very fine chips. The chemical composition of the glass being engraved has an effect both on the texture of the scratch and on the diamond point. The harder the glass the more likely it is that the scratch will be interrupted with relatively larger chips, and also the actual diamond point may be chipped and therefore become useless for normal line work. Many engravers use these chipped diamonds for shading-in large areas. The diamond cannot be resharpened so easily as the steel tip.

Some engravers say that the tungsten carbide steel tipped engraving pencil has the disadvantage of producing a coarser line; and also that the point has to be lifted prior to crossing another already engraved line, as in cross shading (plate 66—fish), for the steel tip is liable to snap off when it jolts through and down into the channel of the already engraved line which it is about to cross. Other engravers say that the point may be allowed to cross another line. W. J. Wilson expresses the opinion that the steel tip has greater potentialities than the diamond, as one can achieve a higher degree of delicacy of line, ranging in one stroke from a very fine to a relatively broad or deep line. The engraver usually holds the tool as he would a pencil, although Laurence Whistler holds the tool in a closed hand.

The design is usually worked out on paper by the artist so that he is able to roughly sketch on the blank the design with a wax pencil. Another method used is to coat the surface of the glass with a mixture of gum arabic and white ink. When this is dry the artist draws the design on this whitened surface with a sharp pointed soft black lead pencil. In both cases the engraver relies on his artistic ability in the engraving of the detail. In the former he fills in the detail by engraving freely, and in the latter he engraves over or through the pencil lines. Most engravers place the blank on a black or very dark, usually velvet, cushion, and place a source of light behind a translucent screen allowing a diffused light to flow into the bowl of the blank. This illuminates the engraved lines, making them translucent and easily visible. In the case of engraving over a pencil line on a white base coating, the light is diffused through the glass and shows up as a translucent bright line surrounded by the duller white of the base coating. The engraved line naturally shows up very well against the 'black mirrored' reverse surface of the glass vessel. The disadvantage of working over a pencil line on white base coating is that the engraver is unable to see the full 'natural' result effect of his work as it progresses. To obtain this the white coating has to be washed off.

Shading and form are produced by engraving oblique, horizontal or vertical lines and cross-hatching, the lines varying in proximity according to the depth or lightness of shading or form effect required. The other method of shading or giving form to a design is to stipple it, which, as has been mentioned above, is to cover the area with dots, the proximity of one dot to its neighbouring dots varying according to the effect required. The closer the dots, as with the engraved line, the lighter or whiter the effect. In stippling, the dots form the highlights, and the untouched glass forms the background, shadow or dark areas. This is very effectively illustrated in plates 52, 53, 57 and 59.

The actual process of engraving is a very simple one of 'scratch-drawing' or stippling on the surface of the glass. The beauty of the technique relies on the skill of the engraver and his artistic abilities, which may be expressed both in a spontaneously created piece of work, represented in plate 61, or in a more meticulous and equally delightful manner, as seen in plates 54 and 67.

To obtain the best effect a glass article has to be displayed well, preferably with a top or bottom light and dark background.

CHAPTER SIX

ENGRAVING GLASS BY COPPER WHEEL

THE WHEEL ENGRAVING of glass is a form of decoration which has been used since Egyptian and Roman times. Roman craftsmen engraved glasses on a lathe using a flint wheel and developed this into flat cutting. Copper-wheel engraving has since been developed in European, Scandinavian and American countries.

Today it is reckoned that it takes five years of apprenticeship to become an engraver. Because of the curvature of the blank, and because the outline of the design has necessarily to be so sketchy, the engraver has of necessity to be a very competent artist, having a knowledge of all forms of art.

Wheel engraving may be divided into three types, as follows :—

(a) *Surface wheel engraving.* The effect here may vary from the very coarse to the exceedingly delicate, according to the skill of the craftsman, the type of wheel used and the effect desired. A stone wheel gives a coarse effect; a copper wheel gives a sharper cut whose delicacy is determined by size; the finer or smaller the wheel, the more delicate the work can be. Practically all modern work is done with a copper wheel.

(b) *Carving in low-relief.* This is done with the wheel and usually polished. The form in the design is produced by the depth of the engraving. This will be explained more fully later.

(c) *Carving in high-relief.* Again the wheel is used, the design being made to stand up from the body of the glass; it is in fact the reverse of carving in low relief. This carving is also usually polished. More about this form of engraving will be written later.

The wheel engraving of glass is then a process whereby (a) the surface of the glass is obscured by fine grinding, as seen in plates 7 and 71; (b) the design is 'modelled' into or ground into the body of the glass vessel, as seen in plates 28 and 73; and (c) the body of the glass vessel is ground away and polished, leaving the design standing upon it (plate 74). The rough surfaces which remain in all cases are very fine in texture. It is difficult to determine the division between surface and low-relief engraving.

I PROPOSE TO discuss surface engraving and carving in low-relief as one form of engraving, and carving in high-relief as another.

As has been mentioned previously, wheel engraving is done with copper wheels mounted by rivets on steel spindles which are inserted in a lathe. The wheels vary in size from a diameter of four inches or

MITRE.   SQUARE.   ROUND.

WHEEL EDGE SHAPES.

Diagram 1

so down to ones as small as a pin's head as seen in plates 75 and 76. The edges of the wheels vary in section from flat to mitre and round (diagram 1) while the thickness of the wheels also vary. A new wheel

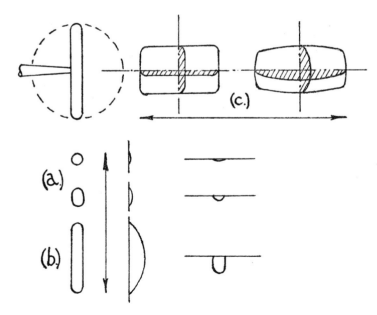

Diagram 2

must be given time to become embedded with emery before it cuts well, the purpose of the copper being to carry the emery into the glass. A well-used wheel will become quite black on its cutting surface. Copper is a relatively soft metal but the discs from which the wheels are to be made may be hardened a little by hammering them. Care must be taken to avoid buckling the wheel, as it would then run out of true when in use.

The glass may be held directly on to the wheel, in which case the round edged wheel will give a round or oval cut when respectively light or heavy pressure is used (diagram 2, a). Alternatively, the glass may be moved in the plane of the wheel's rotation, resulting in long half round sectioned cuts (b). In addition, the glass may be moved across the plane of the wheel's rotation, i.e. in line with the spindle's axis. This gives a much broader cut (c).

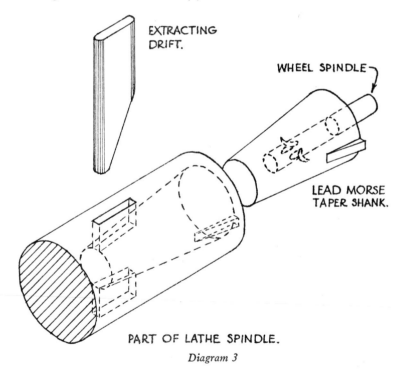

EXTRACTING DRIFT.

WHEEL SPINDLE

LEAD MORSE TAPER SHANK.

PART OF LATHE SPINDLE.

Diagram 3

Some engravers scrape or turn the edge of the wheel true with a piece of sharp hard steel, supported at spindle centre height. When the wheel's edge is ground out of shape it may be reshaped simply by

44

using a fine file on the edge of the revolving wheel. Engraving involves the mastery of some fifty wheels or more, the wheels are changed frequently to suit the type of work being done. Time is saved when work is in progress on an individual piece, or a set of glasses, as the engraver usually completes as many cuts as possible with the one wheel before it is changed for another. For this to be done quickly the spindles are fitted with a lead morse taper sleeve and key which is frictionally held in the lathe shaft, so that the wheels are at a distance of some nine inches from the lathe support or pillar (diagram 3). Originally the lathes were driven by foot, and pulley wheels enabled a variety of spindle speeds to be obtained. Lathes are now driven by electric motors. The speeds are usually kept low, with the range of speeds spaced on either side of about 500 r.p.m., although for different purposes it varies between 150 r.p.m. (large diameter wheel, roughing cuts) and 1,500 r.p.m. (wheel turning and polishing).

To provide the grinding action, abrasive compound is fed on to the wheel by means of a leather tab mounted above the revolving wheel. The tab is either temporarily removed from the wheel in order to be dipped into a dish of abrasive mixture, or the engraver touches the wheel with a finger laden with the mixture. The abrasive is usually emery or carborundum powder; a coarse grit will give too rough a cut and also quickly blunt the copper wheel. Treble washed flour emery can be used provided it is not too fine. A variety of grades of abrasives may be obtained. The abrasive is suspended in a light oil (Colza oil), petroleum and olive oil, or even paraffin, to facilitate the transference of the abrasive from the tab to the wheel's circumference. The oil also allows the ground glass particles to float off, and in addition acts as a coolant.

The design is first of all drawn or painted on the surface of the vessel with 'Chinagraph' pencil or red-lead paint. This drawing is usually very sketchy, owing to the fact that any detail would be ground away. Some engravers prefer to paste a drawing on paper on to the inside surface of the vessel and then work above it, but this method fails when the vessel is necked or very small in diameter. Although the engraver works to a marked design he must have a good sense of draughtsmanship and good artistic ability to be able to portray on a curved surface, flat or other shaped objects. It will be noticed in plates 75 and 76 that the engraver has before him the detailed working drawing of the design he is engraving. This is necessary to ensure accurate work, especially when he is working to another person's design, as he does when he is in industry, and also, as has been stated above, he is unable to have but the briefest of outlines to guide him. Working drawings are illustrated in plates 80 and 82, and the completed glasses in plates 81 and 83 respectively.

The engraver holds the glass vessel with the finger-tips of both hands, and uses his elbows, usually cushioned on felt pads, as pivot-supports. A very great amount of movement, in any desired direction, may be given to the vessel by the engraver through his supple fingers, wrists and elbows.

The vessel is held underneath the wheel, unlike cutting, where the vessel is held on top of the wheel, at a point opposite the engraver's eyes; the engraver in effect 'looks through the wheel' at the point of contact, plates 75 and 76, but *he cannot see* the actual area being engraved at any one moment. The cutting face of the wheel, at work point, moves towards the engraver.

The engraving is done by holding the glass vessel to the wheel so that the latter 'bites' into the surface of the vessel, and then moving the vessel about, in order to grind away the surface. It requires only the slightest touch against the swiftly-rotating wheel to leave a greyish-white mark on the surface of the vessel. This ground away or obscured surface is the pattern or design of surface engraved glass.

If the engraver holds the vessel against the wheel with more pressure a concave ground surface is produced instead of a flat one. This concave surface produces an optical illusion of the design standing in relief, and is known as a low-relief, or 'deep' engraved glass. The deepest point appears to be the nearest to the viewer, and the nearest or shallowest the one farthest away. This technique allows many interesting designs to be carried out, and with the restrained use of polishing —by rouge on wood and cloth—even more varied effects are possible (plates 8, 28 and 73). Acid polished engraving is illustrated in plate 6. The real skill of the craftsman is displayed in his use of this third dimension, and his use of the facilities offered by the process for depicting light and shade effects. In all art mediums a bold, definite, precise statement of the artist's ideas is desirable. In engraving, the best work is achieved when the intended effect is produced by cuts made correctly at the first attempt.

CARVING IN HIGH RELIEF

In carving in high-relief the engraver grinds away the surface of a thick walled vessel leaving certain areas standing above the rest of the new glass surface. These areas are those of the design or decoration.

The ground-away areas are now polished with rouge-smeared wooden wheels, or cork or lead wheels, and finally by cloth wheels. This form of engraving is now extremely rarely practised.

Another, although unconventional, method of engraving by wheel is to accommodate the wheel in a dentist's type hand drill chuck. The tool is used in a similar way to that with which the dentist uses it. The engraver usually holds the glass in his right hand.

This method, it is believed, was first used by a German craftsman some twenty-five years ago, and has been disused until recently, when it was revived and improved upon by Stephen Rickard. David Peace uses a similar method.

The method presents several problems which have to be overcome if it is to be used satisfactorily. If, as in the conventional method of engraving, a pure copper wheel is used, the problems of applying the abrasive to the wheel and cooling the glass blank, heated by the abrasive action of the very swiftly rotating (approx. 3,000 r.p.m.) wheel, have to be solved. The leather tongue feed of oil suspended abrasive cannot be used, as this would hinder the free manipulation of the tool. The only other way of feeding the abrasive is to continually dip the periphery of the wheel into a bath of the abrasive mixture. This can be unsatisfactory because it increases the time taken to complete the decoration and also constantly interrupts the flow of work. The abrasive oil will tend to fly off, due to the centrifugal force at the edge of the quickly rotating wheel. The cooling of the blank can be done by stopping the engraving process until the blank cools, or, as has been done, by allowing a jet of cold water to flow over the blank. This adaptation of the 'normal' copper wheel method is generally an inefficient one, and has been improved upon by craftsmen who use either (a) natural or composition stone wheels, or (b) other special composition grinding wheels, including the diamond dust impregnated wheels. Water in this case is used both as a coolant and as a lubricant to float away the ground glass particles. The only disadvantage is that the stone wears away, and also wears out of shape quickly, and has to be reshaped and renewed often. Some craftsmen use the abrasive wheel dry.

The 'dentist's drill' method allows, by its very nature, and also by its handling properties, a softer and more spontaneous line than the necessarily precise line of the conventional method, the craftsman-artist being allowed to draw freely (plates 10 and 84) and if necessary draw accurately, on the blank. This method, as far as I know, has been used only to surface engrave and carve in low-relief.

John Hutton, who has done much work on the glass screens for the new Coventry Cathedral, uses a much heavier type of hand chuck. The larger wheels are driven by a flexible shaft, as shown in plate 10.

CHAPTER SEVEN

OTHER FORMS OF DECORATION

SANDBLASTING

SANDBLASTING is a comparatively recent invention. Benjamin Tilgham of Philadelphia is credited with the idea in 1870, and his patent extensively covers this method of abrasion.

There is no long tradition of design for sandblasted glass in England or in fact anywhere else. This means that sandblast design can, and does, reflect contemporary ideas, and consequently does not have to keep to traditional forms of design in order to please that portion of the buying public who like traditional design. The sandblast designer is therefore unrestricted, and is able to express himself freely in this form of decoration.

The sandblasting of glass is a process whereby glass is marked or obscured by projecting a jet of abrasive material on to the surface of the glass. The force of impact of the abrasive, chips a fine, granular texture in the natural or polished surface of the glass. The equipment required for this process consists of : an air compressor, a container for abrasive, and a cabin in which the process is carried out and which is fitted with an extraction fan and a window. The jet of abrasive is obtained by allowing the abrasive to fall into a stream of air which passes through a nozzle. The abrasive is carborundum powder or aloxite grit, as the operator is in danger of contracting silicosis if sand is used. Air pressure varies from one to thirty pounds per square inch. The spent abrasive and glass powder is taken away by the extraction fan. The sandblasting is carried out in the cabin with the worker controlling the operation from outside, using the window to view his work, with his hands in specially made gloves and sleeves, which may be part of the actual cabin. A second type of machine directs compressed air across a suction tube from the grit hopper, the grit being sucked up and projected through a nozzle on to the glass. Air pressures required are nought to ten pounds per square inch for shading and matt work, and from fifty to one hundred pounds per square inch for deep work. To control the action of the grit within the limits of a given design a stencil is used to protect the remainder of the glass.

A long-wearing stencil, for the purposes of quantity production, may be made of either metal or rubber. For a more detailed design where only one article is to be decorated, the stencil may be made of a glue-paper resist, which, as it is reasonably cheap may be disposed of after use. Sandblast resist paper is prepared by boiling up a solution of Scotch glue in water with the addition of a small quantity of glycerine. This solution is applied to both sides of a large sheet of blotting paper. The number of coats of glue depends on the amount of wear the paper will eventually be subjected to when blasted. Generally one coat is used for light shaded or peppered work. The quantity of glycerine added will depend on the humidity of the workshop at the time of blasting. The pieces of paper should be soft and pliable.

The tacky resist paper is used to cover the glass vessel so that it forms a skin, just as in covering the vessel with lead foil for acid etching. The mosaic method is usually used. All parts of the glass likely to be affected by the abrasive jet must be covered. The relatively new adhesive-coated plastics, if they are fairly substantial, are very useful as sandblast resists. In practice they are much cleaner to use, cut easily and a crisp edge to the design is obtained. These advantages, at any rate for the producer of small quantities of decorated glass, outweigh the increased cost of the material. The nature of the material permits it to stretch a little, thus allowing it to conform to the shape of the glass. Nevertheless, to obtain effective masking the already mentioned mosaic method of covering the shape must be used.

The duration of the sandblasting operation is surprisingly short. A blast of a second or so results in the glass being obscured. If the jet is allowed to play on the glass for a slightly longer time, deeper modelling is achieved. The size of jet, the grade of grit and the air pressure, all affect the speed of abrasion and also the texture of the obscuration.

A matt surface is produced by applying an even blast over the whole of the design. A peppered surface is obtained by using low air pressure and a minimum quantity of grit in order to obscure partially the glass surface. The transparent quality of the glass is only lightly affected, and due to its rather faint effect the peppered texture is generally used in conjunction with matt or shaded work. A shaded effect is one which has a uniform graduation from a totally obscured to a totally clear surface. This effect is successfully obtained only if careful manipulation of the abrasive jet is used. In conjunction with suitable stencils, modelled or shaded work can be used to give 'form' to a design. Unlike the usually restricted flat tones of acid work, this method can be used with success to give a feeling of depth and form in a design, similar to that given by carving in low-relief in engraving. A modelled or deep *gravé* effect is produced by allowing the abrasive grit to wear away the glass to a considerable depth. The variation in depth is obtained by careful manipulation of the stencil masks and gives the idea, or rather the optical illusion, of positive relief, the deeper the abrased surface the more brought forward or raised it appears.

Sandblasted decorated *art glass* and tableglass is relatively rare because the high cost of equipment bars the average private artist from the use of this process. Sandblasting was used to remove partially the opaque blue flashing of the bent glass dish shown in plate 86. Many commercial firms now use sandblasting as a form of decoration on plate glass and tableware, an example is illustrated in plate 85. They often use metal stencil masks.

ENAMELLING

WIDE RANGES OF ceramic enamels are available commercially, either in firing range, texture or colour, and manufacturers advise on the use of their particular products. There are, for instance, low maturing heat enamels for work on the softer lead crystal glasses, an intermediate range for soda glasses, and a high range for the harder glasses of the boro-silicate type, such as 'Pyrex.' These ranges are divided into 'matt,' 'relief,' 'screening,' 'painting' and 'transfer' enamels. Generally by using suitable enamel medium and thinners for the type of glass to be decorated, good results are obtained. The designs are 'traced' or painted on the outside of the glass vessel, using a copy of the design drawn on paper pressed to the inside surface of the glass. The brush is usually of sable or hog hair.

PAINTING

THE PAINTING OF glass as a form of decoration has been employed since the earliest times, but owing to its indurability there is now little record of it. There was difficulty in rendering the painting permanent even at the time of production. The colour was laid on with some sort of fixative such as varnish. This is known as 'cold painting,' and it appears at intervals throughout history. The painting was probably done by individual independent artists and not by the glass manufacturers.

A transparent colour enamel is termed painting, but the division between the transparent enamel and opaque enamel is difficult to find. The use of transfers carrying *true glass enamels* is widespread as

51

opposed to enamelled glass; however, very few artists paint glass in the impermanent style. Transfers, of not a very secure or permanent nature, are now coming into fashion on cheaper table-ware.

STAINING

THIS IS A method of glass decoration borrowed from the stained glass industry. Staining, using an oxide or chloride of silver, was invented early in the fourteenth century and has been used extensively since. The yellow stain is obtained by firing the glass with finely divided colloidal silver. The colour is secured most easily with potash-lime glasses. With hard glasses there is a tendency for the silver to be deposited metallically. Some firms are at present producing some fine art stained glass.

CUTTING

THE CUTTING OF a glass is the process whereby the surface is gouged or deeply scored. In principle the process is intended to enhance the brilliance and sparkle of the glass. The cut glass acts as numerous polished prisms, which increase the light play, enhancing the 'life' of the glass. The process is done by means of rotating wheels; the object being drawn along them. The cutting process may be divided into four sections : marking, roughing, smoothing and polishing.

The blank is marked out by means of a red lead and turpentine paint, which soon dries. The blank is usually divided into a number of sections as a guide to the design to be cut. The detail is omitted in marking out; just the divisions of the circumference and one or two direction and position lines are all that is required. The design is usually a straight-forward geometrical pattern. If a repeated pattern is used the effect is generally more interesting if an odd number of patterns is used.

The cutting wheels, mounted on steel shafts, were traditionally placed between oak bearings mounted on the sides of a wooden trough. At first the wheels were driven by hand, then by water, and later steam power was employed. The wheels are now driven by a belt from an electric motor, and the shafts are carried in metal bearings.

The shapes and thicknesses of the wheels which can be used vary so that the patterns or cuts vary, too. The shape of the wheel's edge varies from a mitre to round and flat; the angles of the mitre and radii of the round vary according to the wishes of the designer. Naturally the thicker the wheel, the wider the cut, but depth of cut is variable.

A steady downward pressure is required. When a wheel edge-shape is worn out of true it is relatively easy to true it by using a tempered file or wheel dressing tool, to 'turn' the wheel true again.

The first stage of the actual cutting is called roughing. This is actually done with a power-driven metal wheel or mill, on to which is fed an abrasive in solution (emery or sand and water). The blank is held by hand above the wheel and lowered on to the wheel's edge, with its cutting face at work point, moving *away* from the operator. (Conversely, in wheel engraving the cutting face of the wheel is moving towards the operator.) The blank is then manipulated so that the wheel cuts a groove, which is naturally and purposely coarse, in the required position, but shorter and shallower than required of the finished article. This is a time-saving operation and as much work as possible is done with one wheel before it is changed for one of different size and shape. When all such cuts have been made these grooves are smoothed, which is the second process of cutting.

The power smoothing wheel is of stone, either of a composition (carborundum) or natural (sandstone) nature. Clean water drips on to the wheel's periphery and each cut is smoothed with this finer abrasive. The cuts are made the required length, depth and width, and are kept smooth, regular, sharp and clean. Lighter cuts are added without previous marking. The pattern should now be complete in every respect except that the cuts have a fine matt appearance. This smoothing operation is the most skilled one in cutting, as accuracy here is essential. The roughing and smoothing of the cuts is done by the craftsman, who looks through the glass at the point of contact of wheel and glass. Today, practically all the cutting work is done with carborundum wheels of varying degrees of coarseness.

The old method of polishing the cuts was by using wooden wheels of the same shape and size as the smoothing wheels, and using a mixture of pumice, rottenstone and water as a polishing medium. The whole of the previous work had to be laboriously gone over. This time factor, and the fact that the lead oxide of the putty powder is injurious to the health, caused the rapid adoption of the acid polishing system once it had been developed.

After smoothing, the glass is carefully washed, cleaned and dried before being dipped by rubber-gloved hands into the acid, a strong solution of hydrofluoric and sulphuric acid. The glass is kept constantly moving, and after about ten seconds the glass is removed and a white film which has been deposited on the glass washed off with pure water. The glass is again washed before dipping in the acid a second time. The reason for this is because the first dipping slightly polishes the cut surface, but slightly dulls the plain surface, and the second dip brings both surfaces up to the same bright polish.

INTAGLIO

THE EFFECT AS well as the processes and technique, is a halfway stage between wheel engraving and cutting.

A lathe which resembles the one used by the engraver, is used, but instead of copper wheels the spindles carry small cutting stones. These stones are replicas of the cutting stones, only on a scale between cutting and engraving wheels.

The glass to be cut is held under the wheel as in engraving, and exactly the same type of processes are carried out. Intaglio cutting is shallower than normal cutting, allowing greater freedom for the craftsman. Designs and patterns are more intricate than in cutting and less delicate than in wheel engraving; it is, in fact, a compromise between the two. The intaglio cuts are not necessarily polished, but when they are, are polished with wheel or acid according to the design.

CAMEO CUTTING

CAMEO CUTTING is now such an extremely rarely practised craft that it might just as well be called extinct. The greatest piece of glassware produced in this style of decoration was the Portland Vase, already mentioned, and this was followed by the Northwoods' replica of the same vase. The effect produced by cameo cutting may be compared with Wedgwood pottery, the design being left in low relief on the surface of the article, the actual design being of a different colour from the base metal.

Firstly the article is made to the desired shape and while at working heat flashed with another colour metal, that is, coated with a second layer of molten glass, usually white on a blue base, the two metals having the same coefficient of expansion. The design is drawn on the surface of the article with a red lead paint. All large areas of the white flashed glass are removed by large engraving wheels, while the details of the design are engraved with smaller wheels. The thickness of the white glass left as the design, may be varied to give a range from opacity to near transparency, facilitating shaping, form and relief effects.

The method of decoration is practically the same as carving in high-relief, except as has been said, flashed glass is used.

The most modern work which I have been able to find was done by Webb & Sons in 1910. There is, however, some decorated glass of this type produced in France. The use of acid is suggested to have been made to remove unwanted glass, and also to polish the article.

PRESSING

THIS TECHNICALLY is not a form of applied decoration, as are the others included in this chapter, as the decoration is an integral part of the vessel.

The vessels are of open shape such as bowls or dishes. The gatherer brings a supply of glass from the furnace and allows it to flow from the punty into the mould. When sufficient glass has entered the mould the presser shears it off, pushes the mould into position, and by means of a lever brings the plunger into contact with the glass. The lowering of the plunger forces the glass into contact with the base and sides of the mould. The plunger may be smooth or shaped according to the requirements of the design. The exterior of the vessel is formed by the mould proper, and any pattern cut in the mould is impressed upon the molten glass. The upward flow of the glass between mould and plunger is controlled by a top ring. The mould may be of two or more hinged sections, according to the shape of the vessel, facilitating the quick and easy release of the vessel.

In mass-production automatic moulds are employed. These machines are fed with molten glass, press it and allow it to cool, and then eject it in a short space of time. When many vessels of the same design are required the machine is fitted with several moulds equally spaced round a circular table. To maintain a constant supply of glass a continuous melting tank is used. From the tank gobs of hot glass are supplied to the press by feeders. The feeding mechanism ensures that the delivery of the glass synchronises with the revolution of the press. The feeders also pre-form the gobs, their shape assisting speedy pressing. The moulds move round from station to station with a slight pause at each. At the first station the gob is received, and at the second the pressing takes place. Then at a third station the glass is allowed to set, and at the fourth stage the vessel is automatically ejected. The fifth stage allows the mould to cool before once again passing to the first station to receive a fresh gob.

The ejected vessels travel by belt through a fire polishing lehr, which removes rough edges caused by the mould, and through the annealing lehr, before they are finally inspected by hand.

GLOSSARY OF TERMS USED IN THE
GLASS INDUSTRY

Acid Polishing. A method of restoring the brilliance to the parts of glass that have been cut. The glass is dipped in tanks containing acid, usually a mixture of four parts hydrofluoric acid to one part of sulphuric acid. The dipping is brief, and is followed immediately by washing to remove the products of chemical action. Lead-potash glasses and some boro-silicate glasses are particularly suitable for this application.

Annealing. To temper glass by controlled heat and gradual cooling after manufacture, to prevent strain and stress. This term is also used for the heat treatment necessary to fix metallic colours on glass.

Arrissing. The process of removing the sharp edges from glass.

Batch. The mixture of ingredient chemicals used in a single glass-making operation.

Blanks. Glass vessels intended for decoration.

Blown Glass. Glass formed by blowing, usually of the type described as 'mouth-blown.'

Blowing-iron. Tube of steel on which glass is blown to shape by mouth. Four feet six inches long, five-eighths to three-quarters of an inch in diameter, tapering smaller to the mouthpiece and tapering to one inch or more to the nose, or gather, end.

Bullion. The central boss in a sheet of crown glass, or alternatively the disc itself. The punty mark left on hand-made window glass.

Burning-off. Removal of surplus glass and moil by melting off.

Cameo. A glass gem or larger object of more than one layer of glass, the superimposed layer being cut away in part to leave the design in relief on the main body of glass.

Chair. A glass-blower's seat, provided with long arms along which the blow-iron and punty are rotated during the shaping of the glass. It also means the team of glassmakers employed at the furnace.

Chairman. A master glass-blower or head of a chair. Usually an accomplished craftsman of some twenty years' experience.

Cracking-off. Glasses as blown normally have an enclosed form. If, therefore, an open shape is required, part of the glass has to be removed by cracking-off. This is done by scoring the glass with a diamond or tungsten-carbide point at the rim and heating with a fine gas flame. The waste cracks off.

Crizzling. The effect of fine surface cracks on glass, otherwise known as crazing.

Cullet. Broken glass that is suitable for remelting. Only cullet of the same chemical composition is allowed to be used as a flux to aid the melting of the batch. The term was originally confined to the scrap glass collected from the ends of blowing-irons and punties. While on the iron the glass formed a collet or little collar.

Cut Glass. Glass decorated by cutting. 'Smooth' cutting has a slightly opaque appearance. 'Brilliant' cutting has the semblance of the original fire polish fully restored to the cut pattern, either by mechanical or acid polishing.

Diamond-point engraving. Hand decoration of glass with a diamond tool. Similar work is done with a point of specially hardened metal (usually tungsten-carbide) in place of the diamond.

Doghouse. Opening in tank furnace through which materials are fed for melting.

Enamel. A hard, glossy, vitreous coating, in opaque white or colours, which can be fused on to glass, either for decoration or for such purposes as lettering.

Engraving. Decoration of glass by holding the blank against the edge of a small revolving copper wheel. Normally distinguishable from deep-cutting, i.e. cut glass, as engraved lines usually only just break the surface of the glass. Engraved designs are more delicate, intricate and free than cut ones, as the much smaller tool allows greater freedom of movement in a limited space.

Etching. This is a wide term that covers various kinds of treatment to which the surface of the glass is subjected. For purposes of decoration, parts of the glass are protected by wax, resin, or other resists, and the glass is then placed for about ten minutes in a strong solution of hydrofluoric acid. Another use of the term is applied to the process for badging glasses by hydrofluoric acid controlled by stencils.

Fire polishing. A way of bringing back the full brightness of glass by subjecting it to flames that cause incipient surface melting. The term is also applied to the fusing or remelting of the rims of tumblers and other glasses after cracking-off or grinding processes.

Flashing. There are two applications of this term in glassmaking. The first is to describe the operation of spinning a glass glove or cylinder, while still in a plastic state, so that it assumes the form of a flat disc or sheet. The final flattening takes place literally in a flash, so that the word is a very appropriate one. Glass bullions for pseudo-antique windows are made in this way.

The other meaning is that of covering plain glass with a thin layer of coloured glass. This is often done with intense colours such as ruby, or cobalt blue, where any great thickness would make the glass too dark and lacking in translucency. The under layer of the clear glass that carries the film of colour is needed to give sufficient strength to the whole. Flashed glass is used for such different things as wine glasses and stained glass windows—and may be decorated in various ways giving interesting results, such as by engraving.

Flint glass. A term originally used for any kind of colourless glass. Originally calcined flints were incorporated in the formula of the metal.

Footmaker. The third assistant in a glassmaking chair, who is responsible for the gathering and initial blowing of the glass.

Frit. See 'Batch.'

Folded foot. The turned-over edge of the foot of a wineglass. A device for giving extra strength.

Friggers. Small models in glass of a great variety of objects, made by master-glassblowers as mementoes, or by apprentices in their spare time for practice. The word is sometimes used also for an experimental piece or one made to test the skill of a youth.

Gadget. A spring-clip tool, mounted on an iron rod, used for holding the foot of a glass while the body part is being shaped by the glass-maker.

Gaffer. Another name for the head of a chair or team of glassmakers.

Glasshouse. The building in which the glass melting furnaces stand, and in which the actual handling of the molten glass takes place.

Glory-hole. A glassmaker's supplementary furnace. When elaborate glasses are being made by hand the glass becomes too stiff to work before the object is finished. Reheating in the glory-hole then becomes necessary before operations can continue.

Intaglio cutting. A form of decoration for glass that is intermediate between cutting and engraving. Usually polished.

Knop. A variant of 'knob.' An ornamental feature either solid or hollow (the latter sometimes containing a coin) introduced in the stem of a wine glass.

Lehr, Lear, Lier. The tunnel in which glass is annealed.

Marver. The iron slab on which the gathering of molten glass is rolled to give it a symmetrical shape before it is blown.

Metal. A semi-technical term, commonly used for glass in the molten state and less frequently for glass when cold.

Mitre-cut. Cut obtained by using a v-edged abrasive wheel.

Moil. The waste glass left on a blow-iron or punty after use. The term is also applied to the waste glass resulting from the cracking-off process.

Mould. Receptacle in which glass is shaped by blowing or pressing.

Off-hand. A term used to indicate that a glass has been made throughout by hand.

Pot. The fireclay crucible in which the melting of the batch, and remelting of the metal takes place. The furnace is called the Pot Furnace.

Pressed glass. Glassware produced by forcing molten glass into a mould by means of a plunger, etc., as opposed to blowing into shape by air pressure.

Prunt. A moulded glass ornament; also the tool for making it.

Prucellas. A glassmaker's tool shaped like a spring sugar-tongs with shear ends.

Punty, Pontie, Pontil, Ponty, Puntee. An iron rod used for holding glass vessels during manufacture.

Puntying. Grinding away the rough punty mark.

Punty mark. The rough place on the underside of the foot of antique wine glasses, where the glass was attached to the punty during manufacture. To stand well puntied glasses had to have a domed or folded foot.

Servitor. The second man, or chief assistant in a glassmaking chair or team.

Shape. A blank or curved surface, e.g., bowl, jug, wineglass, etc., but not a flat piece or sheet of glass.

Shop. A familiar name for a set of glassmakers and their assistants. A 'wine-shop,' for example, is a team expert in making wineglasses.

Soda-lime glass. A common batch mixture for glass which has as its principal ingredients soda, lime and silica.

Spun glass. Glass thread, originally spun by hand on a revolving wheel. The ancestor of the automatically produced glass fibre of the present day.

Straw-stem. The type of wineglass stem made by drawing out the base of the bowl, so that the bowl and stem are in one piece.

Stuck-shank. The stem of a wineglass when made separately, which shows a joint mark where it has been attached to the bowl and foot.

Tank furnace. A furnace in which the glass is melted in bulk, especially for use with automatic machines, e.g. for bottles, plate and sheet glass.

Taker-in. The youth who takes glasses, immediately they are made, and places them in the annealing lehr. The youngest and/or least experienced member of the chair.

Tool, Glassmaker's. A tool which resembles a pair of tongs shod with wood; used for fashioning blown glass.

Workman. See 'Chairman' or 'Gaffer.'

NOTES TO ILLUSTRATIONS

1. A lovely covered chalice in traditonal style designed and diamond-point engraved by W. J. Wilson. (Permission: W. J. Wilson, F.S.I.A.)

2. A wineglass diamond-point engraved by W. J. Wilson. The hollow knopped stuck-shank contains a coin. The traditional border design complements the traditional shape of the glass. (Permission: W. J. Wilson, F.S.I.A.)

3. An interesting example of modern diamond-point engraving in the style of the eighteenth century, by W. J. Wilson. (Permission: W. J. Wilson, F.S.I.A.)

4. A decanter, goblet and liqueur glass engraved with a barley design. Made of the highest quality full-lead crystal by Thos. Webb & Sons, Stourbridge, and engraved in their decoration shop. (Permission: Council of Industrial Design.)

5. A decanter and goblet designed by Tom Jones for Stevens & Williams Ltd., Stourbridge. (Permission: Council of Industrial Design.)

6. Engraved wines commercially produced by the Stourbridge Glass Co. Ltd. Note that the engraving, as on many antique pieces, has been polished. (Permission: The Stourbridge Glass Co. Ltd., Stourbridge.)

7. The Edinburgh Crystal Glass Co.'s 'Thistle' service, on which engraving and cutting are used to provide the decoration. (Permission: The Edinburgh Crystal Glass Co. Ltd., Edinburgh.)

8. A 12″ high thick crystal vase designed and made by Stuart & Sons, and decorated by them with deep engraving, both matt and polished. Note how the aquatic subject is complemented by the 'liquid' glass. (Permission: Stuart & Sons, Stourbridge.)

9. One of several trophies commissioned by the Shropshire Horticultural Society and made and engraved by Stuart & Sons. (Permission: Stuart & Sons, Stourbridge.)

10. *St. Hilda.* John Hutton at work on one of the engraved glass panels which form the Great West Screen of Coventry Cathedral. To be noted in this plate is the wheel, held in both hands, which is driven through a sheathed flexible shaft by means of the electric motor mounted on the trestle to the left side of the picture. A bracket, attached to the wheel's hand grip, carries a piece of water-saturated cloth to the wheel's periphery. (Permission: Keystone Press Agency Ltd.)

11. *Fountain.* Height 8″. A vase engraved by copper wheel, with the additional use of diamond point (hair and waves), by E. J. Webster. (Permission: E. J. Webster, DES.R.C.A.)

12. *Coronet of Roses*. Diameter 9". Designed and engraved by E. J. Webster. The bee, at the bottom left-hand corner of the decoration in this elevation, illustrates the use which Miss Webster made of polishing wheel-engraved shapes to provide modelling, and then diamond-point engraving them to give detail.
(Permission: E. J. Webster, DES.R.C.A.)

13. A glorious engraved decanter. Height 12". Designed and engraved with copper wheel, by E. J. Webster.   (Permission: E. J. Webster, DES.R.C.A.)

14. *The Merry-Go-Round Bowl*. Designed by Sidney Waugh, the American sculptor; this superb casket-shaped vase of engraved Steuben Glass was President and Mrs. Truman's gift to H.M. The Queen on the occasion of Her Majesty's wedding.   (Permission: Steuben Glass, New York.)

15. *The Mariner's Bowl*. Designed by Sidney Waugh and made and engraved by Steuben Glass. One of Mr. Waugh's most famous pieces, now in the John Herron Art Institute, Indianapolis.   (Permission: Steuben Glass, New York.)

16. *The Dove*. Designed by Robin Darwin, Principal, Royal College of Art, London, and engraved by a craftsman of the Steuben Glass. The plate is of 13" diameter, and is wheel engraved with a delicate linear rendering of a girl with a dove.   (Permission: Steuben Glass, New York.)

17. *Christmas Rose*. Designed by R. Y. Goodden, Professor of the Department of Industrial Glass, Royal College of Art, London, and wheel engraved by a Steuben Glass craftsman. Diameter 14".
(Permission: Steuben Glass, New York.)

18. *Frieze*. Designed by John Piper. Length 19". A decorative plaque formed of clear crystal and engraved with a frieze of dancing girls executed in linear style. Wheel engraved by a Steuben Glass craftsman.
(Permission: Steuben Glass, New York.)

19. *Saying of Confucius*. Crystal style, 7¼" high, engraved with a Confucian saying in formal characters, from a design by a distinguished scholar and poet, Cho Chung-yung. 'Confucius said, "Advance the upright and set aside the crooked, then the people will acquiesce".' The artist's seals are incorporated in the design.   (Permission: Steuben Glass, New York.)

20. *Burmese Royalty*. A covered urn with an ornamental finial, 16" high, engraved with a design by the Burmese artist U. Ohn Lwin.
(Permission: Steuben Glass, New York.)

21. *Spring Festival of Krishna and Radha*. This ornamental plaque, 13¼" high, bears an engraving designed by Rama Maharana of India.
(Permission: Steuben Glass, New York.)

22. *Dawn*. An engraved crystal disk mounted on a wooden base. The piece is 10½" in height. The shape of the base is derived from the high, curving prow and stern of ancient Egyptian ships.   (Permission: Steuben Glass, New York.)

23. Cognac glass in lead crystal, wheel engraved with a heraldic device and the recipient's initials. Designed by the Leerdam Glass School for the Leerdam Glassworks.
(Permission: N. V. Koninklijke Nederlandsche Glasfabriek, Leerdam, Holland.)

24. *Lavabo Bowl* presented to St. Mary's, Stafford. Inscribed in reverse on the outside of the bowl, LAVABO INTER INNOCENTES MENUS MEAS, on one side; and on the other, the response, ET CIRCUMDABO ALTARE TUUM, DOMINI. 'I will wash my hands in innocency, and so I will go unto thine altar, O Lord.' An interesting use of the transparent quality of glass. Designed and engraved by D. B.
Peace. (Permission: D. B. Peace, A.R.I.B.A., A.M.T.P.I.)

25. Engraved goblet presented to the Archbishop of York by the Dean and Canons of Manchester. The goblet was engraved by D. B. Peace. The inscription is engraved in reverse on the further rim of the bowl, so that it may be read from the front, thus again using the transparent nature of the glass. Note the 'space filling' form of the Coat of Arms. The goblet was specially made for the engraver by James Powell & Sons (Whitefriars) Ltd., to the design of W. J. Wilson. (Permission: D. B. Peace, A.R.I.B.A., A.M.T.P.I.)

26. A commemorative pane, commissioned by E. B. Freckingham, Esq., in 1953. Engraved by D. B. Peace. (Permission: E. B. Freckingham, Esq.
Photograph: H. Tempest Ltd., Nottingham.)

26. INSET: The design in detail. (Permission: D. B. Peace, A.R.I.B.A., A.M.T.P.I.)

27. *Fishes.* Part of a water set of wheel-engraved designs executed by Dorothy Brown. (Permission: Dorothy Brown, D.A.[EDIN.])

28. *The Pearl Diver.* Designed by Vicke Lindstrand for A. B. Orrefors Glasbruk. Now in the National Museum, Stockholm.
(Permission: A. B. Orrefors Glasbruk, Sweden.)

29. *Finestra.* Designed by Tapio Wirkkala and wheel engraved by Theodor Käppi for the Karhula-Iittala Glassworks.
(Permission: Karhula-Iittala Glassworks, Finland.)

30. Wheel engraving executed at the S.A.L.I.R. (Studio 'Ars Labor' Industrie Riunite), designed by Frederic Pelzel in 1954. (Permission: S.A.L.I.R., Italy.)

31. Four examples of Danish wheel-engraved glass. Designed by Jacob Bang and engraved by Elving Runemalm, a Swedish engraver, who helped to develop the craft at the Holmegaards Glasvaerk. These pieces were produced between 1934 and 1940. (Permission: Holmegaards Glasvaerk, Denmark.)

32. A dish, copper-wheel and diamond-point engraved by Åse Voss Schrader in 1957. (Permission: Åse Voss Schrader.)

33.   An engraved glass by D. B. Peace in the possession of Brig. and Mrs. J. C. Cunningham. The high quality of the lettering, which in itself is both decorative and commemorative, is particularly noteworthy.
(Permission: D. B. Peace, A.R.I.B.A., A.M.T.P.I.)

34.   'Wine that maketh glad the heart of man.' A decanter engraved by D. B. Peace, and now in the possession of the Manchester City Art Gallery.
(Permission: Manchester City Art Gallery.)

35.   A workman using a blow iron. The glass gather is in a molten condition. Note the construction of the chair and the few simple tools shown.
(Permission: Central Press Photos Ltd.)

36.   A workman using a pearwood 'pat' to shape a dish. The punty to which the dish is attached is being revolved with the left hand.
(Permission: Central Press Photos Ltd.)

37.   A workman shearing off excess glass from a bowl. The glass is still in a very soft condition. The white chalk marks on the side of the chair near the workman's right hand are the tally of production.
(Permission: Central Press Photos Ltd.)

38.   A red-flashed bent glass dish with etched decoration by W. M. Harris, a third year student of the Department of Industrial Glass, at the Royal College of Art, 1960.
(Photograph: W. D. Betts.)

39.   A bent glass dish with the red flash progressively removed with acid to provide the decoration. The work of John Richie, a third year student of the Department of Industrial Glass, at the Royal College of Art, 1960.
(Photograph: W. D. Betts.)

40.   Glass panel, acid etched. Design by F. Meydam of Leerdam Glassworks.
(Permission: N. V. Koninklijke Nederlandsche Glasfabriek, Leerdam, Holland.)

41.   An example of acid-etched decoration, showing the Scottish thistle. The work of Webb Corbett Ltd.   (Permission: Glass Manufacturers' Federation.)

42.   This rugged vase is an interesting example of the combination of the processes of wheel engraving and acid etching. The design was first engraved and then the whole vase was etched. Designed by Kaj Franck, engraved by Theodor Käppi, and acid etched at the Karhula-Iittala Glassworks.
(Permission: Karhula-Iittala Glassworks, Finland.)

43.   Cutting the plate used to reproduce the design which is to be acid etched on a glass.
(Permission: Stevens & Williams Ltd., Stourbridge. Photograph: H. Cartwright.)

44. The paper is removed from the plate after it has been resist-ink printed by pressing.
(Permission: Stevens & Williams Ltd., Stourbridge. Photograph: H. Cartwright.)

45. The transfer of the resist-ink print from the paper support to the surface of the glass.
(Permission: Stevens & Williams Ltd., Stourbridge. Photograph: H. Cartwright.)

46. The application of acid resist paint to the areas of the glass which are not to be acid etched.
(Permission: Stevens & Williams Ltd., Stourbridge. Photograph: H. Cartwright.)

47. The glass is dipped into the acid bath.
(Permission: Stevens & Williams Ltd., Stourbridge. Photograph: H. Cartwright.)

48. The acid-etched glass, finished after the processes shown in plates 43 to 47 inclusive.
(Permission: Stevens & Williams Ltd., Stourbridge. Photograph: H. Cartwright.)

49. The stencil on this waxed glass jug is cut with a steel point.
(Permission: Mr. Thompson. Photograph: H. Cartwright.)

50. Jug acid-etched through a wax mask by Mr. Thompson.
(Permission: Mr. Thompson. Photograph: H. Cartwright.)

51. A diamond point engraved glass, designed and engraved by W. J. Wilson. Note the simple diamond-point engraving tool with which this type of work is done.
(Permission: Glass Manufacturers' Federation.)

52. *Windsor Castle.* One of the goblets presented by H.M. The Queen to the President of France in 1957. This superb example of diamond-point engraving is the work of Laurence Whistler, who also designed the 9″ high goblet which was made for him by James Powell & Sons (Whitefriars) Ltd.
(Permission: Rupert Hart-Davis Ltd.)

53. *The Fairy Palace.* (Based on the Royal Pavilion at Brighton.) The subject has been so masterfully treated that it conveys an aura of fantasy. The goblet, 9″ high, was stipple diamond-point engraved by Laurence Whistler in 1958.
(Permission: Rupert Hart-Davis Ltd.)

54. Laurence Whistler has used many architectural subjects, a large proportion of which have been essays in perspective. An example is this *Interior of the Chapel of Trinity College, Oxford (c. 1690),* which was engraved in 1956. The goblet is the property of the College. (Permission: Rupert Hart-Davis Ltd.)

55. *Trethevy Quoit, Cornwall.* The engraving by Laurence Whistler on this goblet was executed in part by diamond-point and in part by drill. It is of interest to note the two distinct approaches made by the artist to the similar subjects depicted in this plate and in plate 56. Owned by Mr. and Mrs. Robert Hall.
(Permission: Rupert Hart-Davis Ltd.)

56. *Stonehenge.* The sunset is engraved on the far side of the bowl, and the stones on the near side as a transparency. This goblet, now owned by Sir Hugh Dawson, was engraved by Laurence Whistler in 1955.

(Permission: Rupert Hart-Davis Ltd.)

57. Laurence Whistler's portrait of his first wife, Jill Furse, on a wineglass blown to the artist's design. 1958. The property of the artist.

(Permission: Rupert Hart-Davis Ltd.)

58. *Civilization.* Designed by Laurence Whistler and copper-wheel engraved by a craftsman of Steuben Glass. Height 12¾". A crystal vase made in the form of a large goblet; its baluster stem is decorated with applied forms. The piece is copper-wheel engraved with a landscape fantasy of classic ruins. It is interesting to note the bold effect which wheel engraving gives to the design of Laurence Whistler, whose own diamond-point engraving is illustrated in plates 52 to 57 inclusive. (Permission: Steuben Glass, New York.)

59. A diamond-point stipple engraved portrait of Margot Fonteyn, and lettering above, by H. Warren Wilson. (Permission: H. Warren Wilson.)

60. *Tethered Goats.* A 7" diameter plate diamond-point engraved by A. L. Pope. (Permission: A. L. Pope, A.R.C.A., A.R.E.)

61. *Heron Chick.* A diamond-point engraving by A. L. Pope on a vase 8" high. The authentic detail portrayed in this and all his work, combined with his artistic skill, makes A. L. Pope's work so spontaneous and lovely.

(Permission: A. L. Pope, A.R.C.A., A.R.E.)

62. *Lilies.* A 12" vase diamond-point engraved by A. L. Pope. The whole of the decoration is easily seen on the one elevation and is complementary to it.

(Permission: A. L. Pope, A.R.C.A., A.R.E.)

63. Holst's *The Planets* was the theme of the engravings by A. L. Pope on the seven goblets and a decanter presented to Sir Malcolm Sargent by the B.B.C. Symphony Orchestra. The picture shows the decanter and one of the goblets, 'Venus.' (Permission: THE TIMES.)

64. A tankard, diamond-point engraved by E. M. Dinkel, R.W.S.

(Permission: Topical Press Agency Ltd.)

65. *Marine Shells.* Sherry glasses, diamond-point engraved by E. M. Dinkel, R.W.S. E. M. Dinkel is now more famous for his diamond-point engraving than for his wheel engraving (see plate 83). (Permission: Topical Press Agency Ltd.)

66. *A Fish.* Diamond-point work in line and stipple by the late Gertrude Bohnert, of Lucerne, Switzerland. Gertrude Bohnert was ranked by many as the finest diamond-point engraver on the continent. She was self-taught.

(Permission: Hans Erni.)

67. Detail, from a large flat fish, of diamond-point engraving by Gertrude Bohnert. (Permission: Hans Erni.)

68. *The Bat.* A diamond-point engraved dish by Gertrude Bohnert. (Permission: Hans Erni.)

69. Crystal dish, diamond-point engraved by W. Heesen of Leerdam Glassworks. Mr. Heesen instigated the revival of diamond-point engraving in Holland.
(Permission: N. V. Koninklijke Nederlandsche Glasfabriek, Leerdam, Holland.)

70. Diamond-point engraved glassware designed by Tono Zancanaro and engraved at the S.A.L.I.R. (Studio 'Ars Labor' Industrie Riuniti), in 1952. (Permission: S.A.L.I.R., Italy.)

71. A tumbler engraved by Stephen Rickard. (Permission: Stephen Rickard, A.R.B.S.)

72. *Tree of Life.* Engraved by Stephen Rickard. (Permission: Stephen Rickard, A.R.B.S.)

73. *Eastern Dancer.* Vase designed for A. B. Orrefors Glasbruk, by Simon Gate (1883-1945). Copper-wheel engraved. (Permission: A. B. Orrefors Glasbruk, Sweden.)

74. *Mother and Child.* Engraved in high-relief to a design by Sven Palmqvist for A. B. Orrefors Glasbruk. (Permission: A. B. Orrefors Glasbruk, Sweden.)

75. A wheel engraver putting the finishing touches on a bowl, one of eleven pieces making up the AMERICAN BALLAD series. The lathe is of traditional style, driven by belt from a motor above. The arm at the top of the lathe carries the leather tab which supplies the wheel with abrasive. The stand in the background contains a range of engraving wheels of various diameters, thicknesses and edge shapes. Note the lead morse taper shanks of the wheels/spindles in the rack, the working drawing behind the lathe, and the elbow pads used by the engraver. It may be seen that the engraver must see 'through the wheel' to achieve his work. (Permission: Steuben Glass, New York.)

76. A modern electrically driven wheel engraving lathe. The piece of glass is *Cinderella*, designed by Sven Palmqvist for A. B. Orrefors Glasbruk, in 1955. Thick Vase 9¾" high. (Permission: A. B. Orrefors Glasbruk, Sweden.)

77. Copper-wheel engraving by Helen Monro on a crystal glass made by James Powell & Sons (Whitefriars) Ltd. (Permission: Council of Industrial Design.)

78. One of a set of wheel-engraved crystal table goblets entitled *Wayside,* designed and engraved by Harold Gordon in 1949 and still in current production. Height 6″, diameter 3½″. This design is also engraved on other shapes or goblets.   (Permission: Council of Industrial Design.)

79. *Trout Fly and Cast.* A crystal tumbler wheel engraved by Harold Gordon. Designed and first produced in 1957.
      (Permission: Council of Industrial Design.)

80. Working elevation and design by J. C. Downing. The completed vase is shown in plate 81 (left).   (Permission: J. C. Downing, A.R.C.A., F.R.S.A.)

81. *Left*: The completed glass of the drawing shown in plate 80.
    Right: A vase decorated by wheel engraving.
      (Permission: J. C. Downing, A.R.C.A., F.R.S.A.)

82. Working elevation and design by E. M. Dinkel, for the wheel-engraved piece shown in plate 83.   (Permission: E. M. Dinkel, R.W.S.)

83. The completed glass of the drawing shown in plate 82.
      (Permission: E. M. Dinkel, R.W.S.)

84. *Three Sprigs.* Engraved by Stephen Rickard on Swedish half-crystal glass.   (Permission: Stephen Rickard, A.R.B.S.)

85. A piece of sandblast decorated table glass. The tumbler was made by Webb Corbett.   (Permission: Glass Manufacturers' Federation.)

86. Sandblasting was used to remove partially the opaque blue flashing of this bent glass dish. The work of W. M. Harris, a third year student of the Department of Industrial Glass, at the Royal College of Art, 1960.
      (Photograph: W. D. Betts.)

1. Chalice, diamond-point engraved by W. J. Wilson, F.S.I.A.
    (courtesy: the artist).

Text engraved on glass: Brigadier SIR JOHN HUNT Everest Expedition 1953

2. Wineglass, diamond-point engraved by W. J. Wilson, F.S.I.A. (courtesy: the artist).

3. Wineglass, diamond-point engraved by W. J. Wilson, F.S.I.A.
(courtesy: the artist).

4. A decanter, goblet and liqueur glass engraved by Thos. Webb & Sons (courtesy: Council of Industrial Design).

5. A decanter and goblet designed by Tom Jones for Stevens & Williams Ltd. (courtesy: Council of Industrial Design).

6. Engraved wineglasses by Stourbridge Glass Co. Ltd. (courtesy: Stourbridge Glass Co. Ltd.)

7. *Thistle* service, engraved and cut, by Edinburgh Crystal Glass Co. Ltd. (courtesy: Edinburgh Crystal Glass Co. Ltd.).

8. Engraved crystal glass by Stuart & Sons (courtesy: Stuart & Sons).

9. Trophy, engraved by Stuart & Sons (courtesy: Stuart & Sons).

10. John Hutton at work on *St. Hilda*, one of the engraved glass panels which form the Great West Screen of Coventry Cathedral (photo: Keystone Press Agency Ltd.).

11. *Fountain.* Vase engraved by copper wheel by E. J. Webster, DES.R.C.A.
(courtesy: the artist).

12. *Coronet of Roses*. Designed and engraved by E. J. Webster, DES.R.C.A.
(courtesy: the artist)

13. Decanter. Designed and engraved with copper wheel by E. J. Webster, DES.R.C.A. (courtesy: the artist).

14. *Merry-Go-Round Bowl*. Designed by Sidney Waugh (courtesy: Steuben Glass).

15. *The Mariner's Bowl.* Designed by Sidney Waugh (courtesy: Steuben Glass).

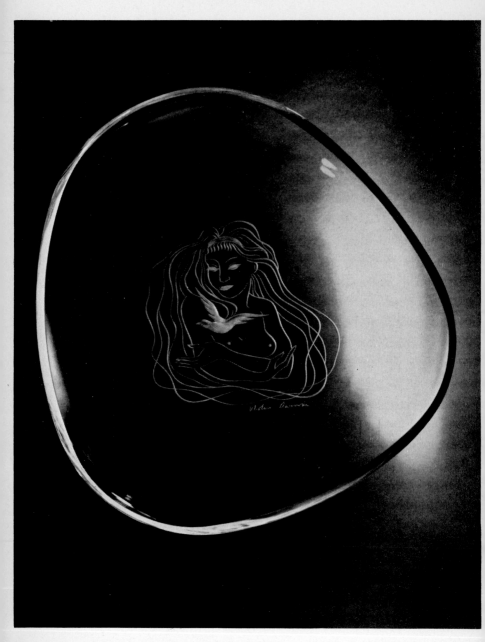

16. *The Dove.* Designed by Robin Darwin, Principal, Royal College of Art.
(courtesy: Steuben Glass).

17. *Christmas Rose*. Designed by Professor R. Y. Goodden, Royal College of Art (courtesy: Steuben Glass).

18. *Frieze*. Designed by John Piper (courtesy: Steuben Glass).

孔子曰舉直
諸枉則民服
卓君庸書

19. *Saying of Confucius.* Crystal, engraved by Steuben Glass (courtesy: Steuben Glass).

20. *Burmese Royalty*. A covered urn, design by U. Ohn Lwin (courtesy:
Steuben Glass).

ing Festival of Krishna and Radha. Plaque designed by Rama Maharana
(courtesy: Steuben Glass).

22. *Dawn.* An engraved crystal disk (courtesy: Steuben Glass).

23. Cognac glass in lead crystal, wheel engraved, designed by the Leerdam Glass School (courtesy: N. V. Koninklijke Nederlandsche Glasfabriek).

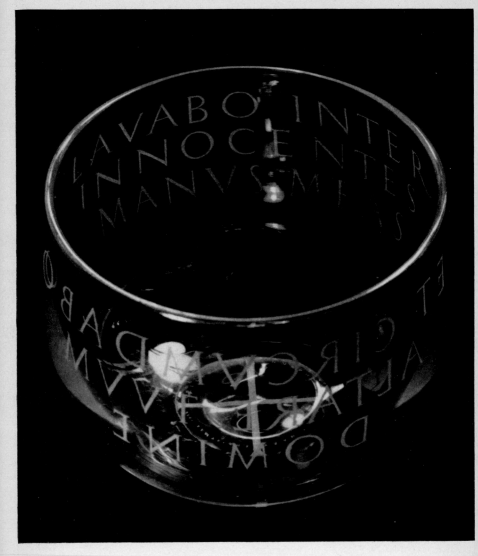

24. *Lavabo Bowl.* Designed and engraved by D. B. Peace, A.R.I.B.A., A.M.T.P.I. (courtesy: the artist).

The Most Reverend the Lord Archbishop of York
MANCHESTER CATHEDRAL
11th September 1957

25.   Goblet engraved by D. B. Peace, A.R.I.B.A., A.M.T.P.I. (courtesy: D. B. Peace).

26. A commemorative pane engraved by D. B. Peace, A.R.I.B.A., A.M.T.P.I. (photo: H. Tempest Ltd.).

27. *Fishes.* Wheel-engraved design by Dorothy Brown, D.A.(EDIN.) (courtesy: the artist).

28. *The Pearl Diver*. Designed by Vicke Lindstrand for A. B. Orrefors Glasbruk (courtesy: A. B. Orrefors Glasbruk).

29. *Finestra*. Designed by Tapio Wirkkala, wheel
engraved by Theodor Käppi (courtesy: Karhula-
Iittala Glassworks).

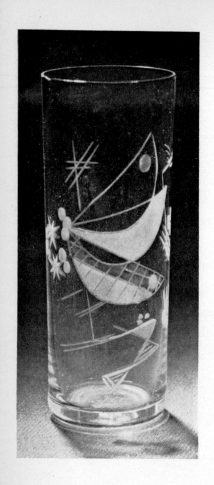

30. Designed by Frederic Pelzel, wheel engraved by 'Ars Labor' studio
(courtesy: S.A.L.I.R., Italy).

31. Designed by Jacob Bang, engraved by Elving Runemalm for Holmegaards
(courtesy: Holmegaards Glasvaerk).

32. A dish, copper wheel and diamond-point engraved by Åse Voss Schrader (courtesy: Karhula-Iittala Glassworks and the artist).

33. An engraved glass by D. B. Peace, A.R.I.B.A., A.M.T.P.I. (courtesy: the artist).

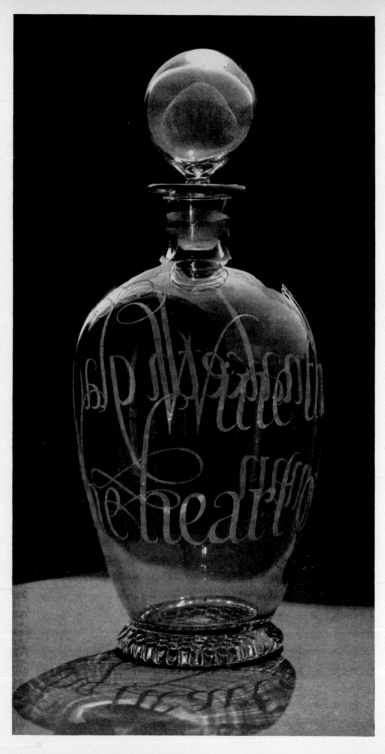

34. Engraved decanter by D. B. Peace, A.R.I.B.A., A.M.T.P.I.
(courtesy: Manchester City Art Gallery).

35. A workman using a blow iron (courtesy: Central Press Photos Ltd.).

36. A workman using a pearwood 'pat' to shape a dish (courtesy: Central Press Photos Ltd.).

37. A workman shearing off excess glass from a bowl (courtesy: Central Press Photos Ltd.).

38. Glass dish with etched decoration by W. M. Harris, Royal College of Art
(photo: W. D. Betts).

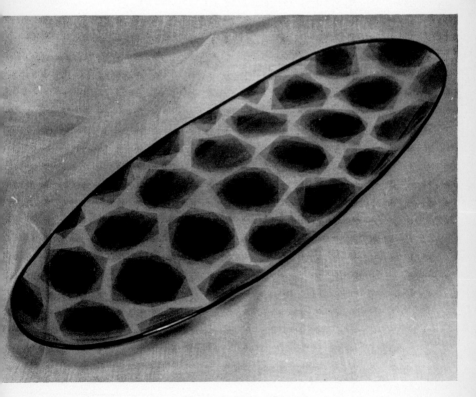

39. Glass dish etched by John Richie, Royal College of Art (photo: W. D. Betts).

40. Glass panel, acid etched. Design by F. Meydam of Leerdam Glassworks
(courtesy: N. V. Koninklijke Nederlandsche Glasfabriek).

41. An example of acid-etched decoration, by Webb Corbett Ltd. (courtesy: Glass Manufacturers' Federation).

42. Vase designed by Kaj Franck, engraved by Theodor Käppi, acid etched at the Karhula-Iittala Glassworks (courtesy: Karhula-Iittala Glassworks).

43. Cutting the plate used to reproduce the design which is to be acid etched on a glass (courtesy: Stevens & Williams Ltd., Stourbridge; photo: H. Cartwright).

46. The application of acid resist paint to the areas of the glass which are not to be acid etched (courtesy: Stevens & Williams Ltd.; photo: H. Cartwright).

47.   The glass is dipped into the acid bath (courtesy: Stevens & Williams Ltd.;
photo: H. Cartwright).

48. The acid-etched glass, finished after the processes shown in plates 43 to 47 inclusive (courtesy: Stevens & Williams Ltd.; photo: H. Cartwright).

49. The stencil on this waxed glass jug is cut with a steel point (courtesy:
Mr. Thompson; photo: H. Cartwright).

50. Jug, acid etched through a wax mask, by Mr. Thompson
(courtesy: Mr. Thompson; photo: H. Cartwright).

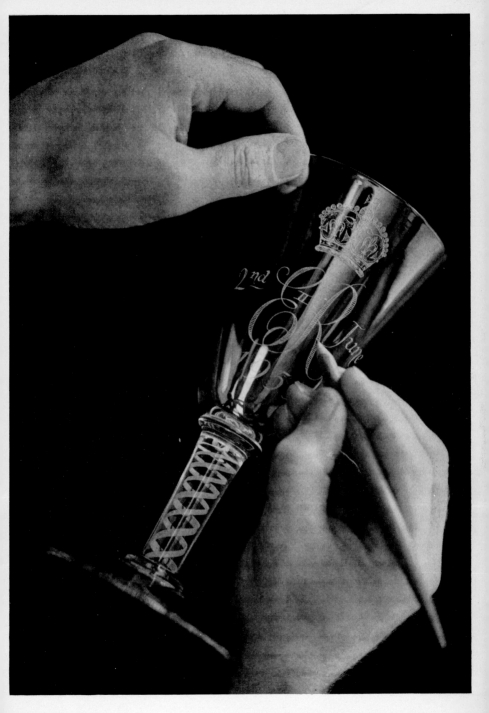

51. A diamond-point engraved glass, designed and engraved by W. J. Wilson
(courtesy: Glass Manufacturers' Federation).

52. *Windsor Castle*. Goblet diamond-point engraved by Laurence Whistler
(courtesy: Rupert Hart-Davis Ltd.).

53. *The Fairy Palace*. Goblet, with stipple diamond-point engraving, by Laurence Whistler (courtesy: Rupert Hart-Davis Ltd.).

54. *Interior of Trinity College Chapel, Oxford c. 1690.* Goblet, engraved by Laurence Whistler (courtesy: Rupert Hart-Davis Ltd.).

55. *Trethevy Quoit, Cornwall.* Engraved part by diamond-point and part by drill by Laurence Whistler (courtesy: Rupert Hart-Davis Ltd.).

56. *Stonehenge*, by Laurence Whistler (courtesy: Rupert Hart-Davis Ltd.).

57. Laurence Whistler's portrait of his first wife, Jill Furse (courtesy: Rupert Hart-Davis Ltd.).

58. *Civilization.* Designed by Laurence Whistler, copper-wheel engraved by Steuben Glass (courtesy: Steuben Glass).

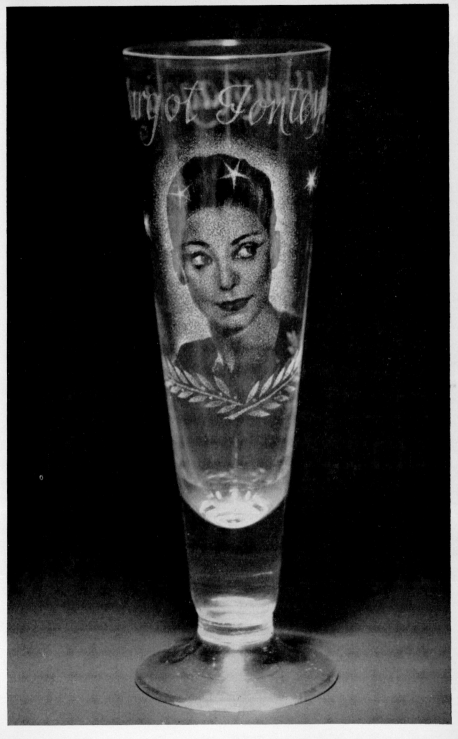

59.   Diamond-point stipple engraved portrait of Margot Fonteyn by H. Warren
Wilson (courtesy: the artist).

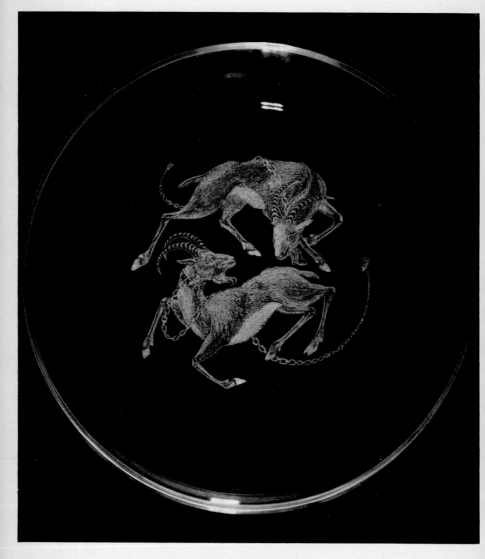

60. *Tethered Goats*. Diamond-point engraved by A. L. Pope, A.R.C.A., A.R.E. (courtesy: the artist).

61. *Heron Chick*. Diamond-point engraved by A. L. Pope, A.R.C.A., A.R.E. (courtesy: the artist).

62. *Lilies*. Diamond-point engraved by A. L. Pope,
A.R.C.A., A.R.E. (courtesy: the artist).

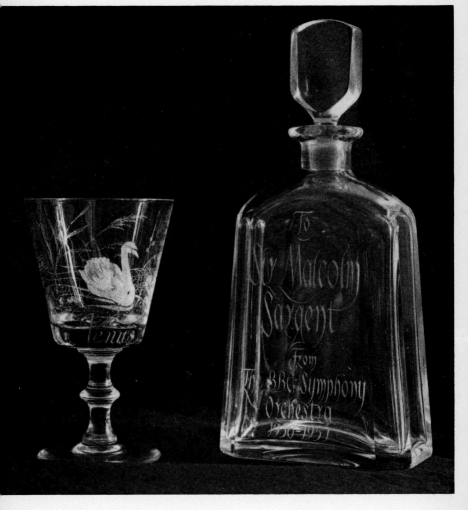

63. Holst's *The Planets*. Decanter and one of the goblets, by A. L. Pope,
A.R.C.A., A.R.E. (courtesy: THE TIMES).

64. A tankard, diamond-point engraved by E. M. Dinkel, R.W.S. (courtesy: Topical Press Agency Ltd.)

65. *Marine Shells*. Sherry glasses, diamond-point engraved by E. M. Dinkel, r.w.s. (courtesy: Topical Press Agency Ltd.).

66. A Fish. Diamond-point engraved by Gertrude Bohnert (courtesy: Hans Erni).

67. Detail, from a large flat dish, of diamond-point engraving by Gertrude Bohnert (courtesy: Hans Erni).

68. *The Bat*. A diamond-point engraved dish by Gertrude Bohnert (courtesy: Hans Erni).

69. Crystal dish, diamond-point engraved by W. Heesen (courtesy: N. V.
Koninklijke Nederlandsche Glasfabriek).

70. Diamond-point engraved glassware designed by Tono Zancanaro and engraved by 'Ars Labor' studio (courtesy: S.A.L.I.R.).

71. A tumbler engraved by Stephen Rickard, A.R.B.S. (courtesy: the artist).

72. *Tree of Life*. Engraved by Stephen Rickard, A.R.B.S. (courtesy: the artist).

73. *Eastern Dancer*. Vase designed by Simon Gate for A. B. Orrefors Glasbruk (courtesy: A. B. Orrefors Glasbruk).

74. *Mother and Child*, by Sven Palmqvist, engraved in high relief by A. B. Orrefors Glasbruk (courtesy: A. B. Orrefors Glasbruk).

75. A wheel engraver putting the finishing touches to a bowl (courtesy: Steuben Glass).

76. A modern electrically driven wheel engraving lathe (courtesy: A. B. Orrefors Glasbruk).

77. Copper-wheel engraving by Helen Monro on a crystal glass made by James Powell & Sons (courtesy: Council of Industrial Design).

78. One of a set of wheel-engraved crystal table goblets by Harold Gordon (courtesy: Council of Industrial Design).

79. *Trout Fly and Cast.* A crystal tumbler wheel engraved by Harold Gordon
(courtesy: Council of Industrial Design)

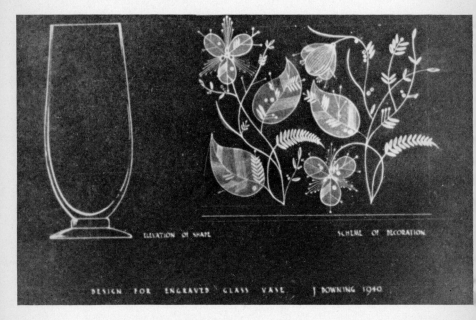

ELEVATION OF SHAPE   SCHEME OF DECORATION

DESIGN FOR ENGRAVED GLASS VASE   J DOWNING 1940

80. Working elevation and design by J. C. Downing, A.R.C.A., F.R.S.A. See pl. 81 (courtesy: the artist).

81. *Left*: The completed glass of the drawing shown in plate 80.
Right: A vase decorated by wheel engraving (courtesy: J. C. Downing).

82. Working elevation and design by E. M. Dinkel, R.W.S. See pl. 83
(courtesy: the artist).

83.   The completed glass of the drawing shown in plate 82
(courtesy: E. M. Dinkel).

84. *Three Sprigs*. Engraved by Stephen Rickard, A.R.B.S. (courtesy: the artist).

85. A piece of sandblast decorated table glass. Tumbler by Webb Corbett
(courtesy: Glass Manufacturers' Federation).

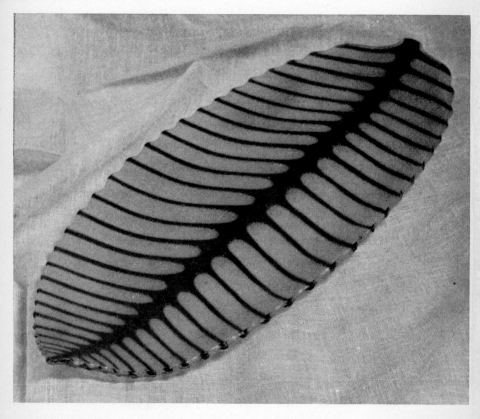

86. Sandblasting was used to remove partially the opaque blue flashing. Work
of W. M. Harris, Royal College of Art (photo: W. D. Betts).